Praise for All Seasons

The hymns of
James Quinn SJ

T0316227

GEOFFREY
CHAPMAN

Geoffrey Chapman
A Cassell imprint
Villiers House, 41/47 Strand, London WC2N 5JE

First published 1994

British Library Cataloguing-in-Publication Data
A catalogue record for this book is available from the British Library.

ISBN 0-225-66715-0

Printed and bound in the United States of America.

Contents

Hymns for the Church Year

O Child of Promise, Come!
SM

O Child of promise, come!
O come, Emmanuel!
Come, prince of peace, to David's throne;
come, God with us to dwell!

The Lord's true Servant, come,
in whom is his delight,
on whom his holy Spirit rests,
the Gentiles' promised light!

O come, anointed One,
to show blind eyes your face!
Good tidings to the poor announce;
proclaim God's year of grace!

O man of sorrows, come,
despised and cast aside!
O bear our griefs, and by your wounds
redeem us from our pride!

O come, God's holy Lamb;
to death be meekly led!
O save the many by your Blood,
for sin so gladly shed!

O come, Messiah King,
to reign in endless light,
when heav'nly peace at last goes forth
from Zion's holy height!

O Come, O Come, Thou Child Emmanuel
10 10 10 10 10 10

O come, O come, thou child Emmanuel,
to free thy people, captive Israel!
From exile lead them home, thou promised one
so long awaited, God's beloved Son!
Rejoice, rejoice, the child Emmanuel
shall soon be born to save thee, Israel!

O come, O come, thou shoot of Jesse's tree!
Thy downcast people from their bonds set free!
Thy loved ones rescue from their deadly foe;
Save them from evil and from every woe!

O come and rise, thou Dayspring, in the sky!
Come, shine on us who deep in shadows lie!
Come, radiant Dawn, to end sin's weary night;
the clouds of gloom for ever put to flight!

O come, thou Key of David's city fair!
Unlock its gates and bid us enter there!
Make straight our path to realms of bliss above;
from loss of thee, O save us by thy love!

O come, O come, who art the Lord most high,
who didst of old come down on Sinai
to give thy law in sight of Israel
in wondrous splendor, come, Emmanuel!

Text: James Quinn, SJ, ©.
Possible Tune: SANDYS, LITTLE MARLBOROUGH, CAMBRIDGE
Scripture References: Isaiah 2:2-5; 7:14; 9:6-7; 42:1-7,
    53:1-12; 61:1-2
Topics: Advent, Deliverance, Peace (for the world),
    Redemption, Return of Christ, Salvation

Text: *Veni, veni, Emmanuel*, Latin, ca. 9th cent.;
    trans. by James Quinn, SJ, ©.
Possible Tune: VENI, EMMANUEL
Topics: Advent

God the Father Sends His Angel

87 87

God the Father sends his angel
from his throne in heav'n above;
when the angel speaks to Mary,
Mary's heart is full of love.

Gabriel says: "Rejoice, O Mary,
full of grace: the Lord is near.
You will bear God's Son, O Maiden:
God has promised, have no fear."

Mary says: "I am God's servant;
I will keep his holy word;
I will gladly be the Mother
of my Savior and my Lord."

Now the Spirit overshadows
God the Father's chosen one:
She becomes the Maiden-Mother
of the Father's only Son.

God the Word, the Father's Wisdom,
comes on earth as Mary's child:
God, our glory, shines among us;
God with us is reconciled.

Praise the Father, fount of blessing;
praise his Son, whom Mary bore;
praise the Lord of life, the Spirit;
praise one God for evermore.

Text: James Quinn, SJ, 1988, ©.
Possible Tune: EVENING PRAYER
Topics: Advent, Annunciation, Mary

Look Down from Heaven, Lord

11 11 11 with refrain

Look down from heaven, Lord, with eyes of pity;
stretch our your hand in forgiveness.
  Jesus, God's Firstborn, glory born of glory,
  Word of the Father, turn to us in mercy;
  come to our rescue, come, eternal Wisdom.

Look down from heaven, Lord, with eyes of pity;
stretch our your hand in forgiveness.
  Son born to save us, heir of David's kingdom,
  promised Messiah, crucified Redeemer,
  King of compassion, reign in peace among us.

Look down from heaven, Lord, with eyes of pity;
stretch our your hand in forgiveness.
  Jesus, our Daystar, Lord of earth and heaven,
  Joy of the angels, Priest of all creation,
  come in your glory, come again, Lord Jesus.

Text: James Quinn, SJ, ©.
Possible Tune: ATTENDE, DOMINE
Topics: Advent, Salvation

Of the Firstborn of the Father

87 87 87 with refrain

Of the firstborn of the Father,
loved before time's dawn, we sing:
alpha, fount of all creation,
omega, its glorious King!
What has been, what is, what will be,
to its Lord in homage bring,
as before, so evermore!

This is he whom ancient seers
through the mists of time foretold,
he the Child revealed by prophets
in the sacred books of old!
Promised heir of all the ages,
by all ages be extolled.
As before, so evermore!

Hail the morn of wondrous gladness,
dawn of blessing for our race,
when the Bride of God the Spirit
bears the promised Child of grace!
Tiny Child, yet world's Redeemer,
O what joy to see your face,
now at last and evermore!

Glory to the loving Father,
glory to his only Son,
to the Spirit, equal glory,
persons three, yet Godhead one!
Glory be from all creation
to one God while ages run
evermore and evermore!

Town of David, King and Shepherd

87 87

Town of David, King and Shepherd,
now has come your promised hour,
when the lowly branch of Jesse
blossoms into glorious flower.

Full of joy, the Virgin-Mother
now will bring her Lord to birth,
Son of God and Son of Mary,
God with us, a Child on earth.

After sin's long night of triumph
Christ will dawn as endless day:
light of light, to heaven's glory
he will guide our pilgrim way.

Sinless, he will die for sinners;
wounded, he will be our peace;
poor, he will reward with riches;
captive, he will bring release.

Glory be to God the Father,
glory be to Mary's Child,
glory be to God the Spirit:
God with us is reconciled.

Text: *Corde natus ex parentis*, Prudentius (348-413);
    para. by James Quinn, SJ, ©.
Possible Tune: DIVINUM MYSTERIUM
Topics: Christmas

Text: James Quinn, SJ, ©.
Possible Tunes: WALTHAM, TOWN OF DAVID (Held)
Topics: Biblical names (Bethlehem), Christmas, Light,
    Salvation

3

Before All Creation the Word Had Been Born
11 11 11 11

Before all creation the Word had been born,
with God ever dwelling, the Word that was God.
before the beginning, when time was not yet,
the Word that was Wisdom was dwelling with God.

The Word was the Maker of all that was made;
in him was the life that enlightens the world.
The light shines in darkness, and darkness is gone;
the night could not conquer the light that was life.

The Word was the true light that shines on us all.
The world knew him not, though he dwelt in the
    world;
the world of his making its Maker disowned;
his own world he entered unwelcomed, unknown.

To all who received him by faith in his name
his gift was the power to be children of God,
of blood not begotten, nor will of the flesh,
nor human desiring, but only of God.

The Word took our nature and dwelt in our midst,
the presence of God in his temple of flesh.
We saw him in glory as God's only Son,
in whom is the fullness of grace and of truth.

Text: James Quinn, SJ, 1988, ©.
Possible Tune: COLUMCILLE
Scripture Reference: John 1:1-5, 9-14
Topics: Christmas, Word of God

Angel Voices, Richly Blending
88 87

Angel voices, richly blending,
shepherds to the manger sending,
sing of peace from heav'n descending!
Shepherds, greet your Shepherd-King!

Lo! a star is brightly glowing!
Eastern kings their gifts are showing
to the King whose gifts pass knowing!
Gentiles, greet the Gentiles' King!

To the manger come adoring,
hearts in thankfulness outpouring
to the Child, true peace restoring,
Mary's Son, our God and King!

Text: *Quem pastores laudavere*, adapt. from the 14th
    cent. text by James Quinn, SJ, ©.
Possible Tune: QUEM PASTORE LAUDAVERE
Scripture references: st. 1: Luke 2:8-14; st. 2: Psalm 89
    (88):19-37, Isaiah 7:14, Matthew 2:1-12, Psalm 72
    (71):10-11, Numbers 24:17
Topics: Christmas

Children, Greet Your New-Born King
78 88

Children, greet your new-born King,
around his crib your carol sing!
He sleeps and smiles, a Child so small,
yet he is King and Lord of all!

Angels fill the skies with song
for him to whom the skies belong!
They sing of peace on Christmas morn,
for now the Prince of Peace is born!

Mary sings her lullaby,
while Joseph stands with watchful eye;
the shepherds kneel before their King,
and kings from far their gifts will bring!

Children, sing with voices clear,
and greet your new-born Savior dear!
He is the Lord of heaven above,
now born a Child to win our love!

Text: James Quinn, SJ, ©.
Possible Tune: LUINNEACH
Topics: Christmas

Skies at Midnight Burst Asunder
866 866

Skies at midnight burst asunder!
All is light,
angels bright
sing while shepherds wonder:
"Glory be to God in heaven!
Peace on earth
by Christ's birth
now at last is given!"

Songs of old, O Child, foretold you!
Promised One,
David's Son,
virgin's arms enfold you!
Kings with gifts will kneel before you!
Jacob's star
from afar
leads them to adore you!

Banished now is all our sadness!
On this morn
Christ is born,
sing new songs of gladness!
Praise your Lord, O all creation!
Joys untold
now unfold,
sing in jubilation!

Text: James Quinn, SJ, ©.
Possible Tune: BONN (WARUM SOLLT' ICH)
Scripture References: Isaiah 7:14, Matthew 2:1-12,
    Luke 2:8-14
Topics: Christmas

Come, Joyful Pilgrims
Irregular

Come, joyful pilgrims, come with songs of
    gladness,
come to the manger where Jesus is laid!
New-born behold him, King of heaven's angels!
O come in adoration, O come in adoration,
O come in adoration to Christ the Lord!

True God from true God, light from light eternal,
Maiden for Mother, is born for us all,
only-begotten Son of God the Father:
O come in adoration, O come in adoration,
O come in adoration to Christ the Lord!

Shepherds, invited by the choirs of angels,
haste to the manger to welcome the Lord!
Eagerly follow in the shepherd's footsteps:
O come in adoration, O come in adoration,
O come in adoration to Christ the Lord!

Led by the wondrous star that went before them,
kings give in homage gold, incense, and myrrh!
Come now and give him all our heart's devotion:
O come in adoration, O come in adoration,
O come in adoration to Christ the Lord!

Glory of Godhead, splendor uncreated,
here lies in hiding, concealed in a Child!
Flesh in its frailty veils the Lord almighty:
O come in adoration, O come in adoration,
O come in adoration to Christ the Lord!

Straw for his bedding, he is poor and homeless;
cherish and warm him in welcoming arms!
If he so loved us, who can love refuse him?
O come in adoration, O come in adoration,
O come in adoration to Christ the Lord!

Angels in chorus, greet the new-born Savior,
sing in his honor hosannas on high!
Glory to God be in the highest heaven:
O come in adoration, O come in adoration,
O come in adoration to Christ the Lord!

Sing to the Christ-Child, born on Christmas
    morning!
Now and for ever may Jesus be praised,
Word of the Father made for us incarnate.
O come in adoration, O come in adoration,
O come in adoration to Christ the Lord!

Text:*Adeste, fideles,* John Francis Wade (1711-1786);
trans. by James Quinn, SJ, ©.
Possible Tune: ADESTE FIDELES
Topics: Christmas

See in David's City

66 66 with refrain

See in David's city
child in manger lowly,
come from heav'n in pity,
Christ the Lord all-holy.
Refrain
    Heaven is ringing;
    angels are winging,
    joyfully singing,
    glad tidings bringing:
    Gloria, gloria, gloria in excelsis Deo.

King of all creation,
earthly throne a manger,
he is our salvation,
through to us a stranger.
    Refrain

Shepherds bow before him,
see, he smiles his pleasure;
Eastern kings adore him,
leave with him their treasure.
    Refrain

Sleep, Little Child, While You May

77 77D with refrain

Sleep, little Child, while you may,
warm in your cradle of hay.
Sleep in the silence of night,
rest till the dawning of light.
Glory has greeted your birth,
peace has come down upon earth.
Sleep, little Child, do not fear:
Mary, your Mother, is near.
So sleep, while you may!

Smile, little Child, in your sleep:
Joseph his night-watch will keep.
Silent, he waits for the day,
keeping all danger at bay.
Guardian most faithful and true,
fondly he gazes on you.
Sleep, little Child, do not fear:
Joseph, so loving, is near.
So sleep, while you may!

Sleep, little Child, all is well:
shepherds with wonders to tell
come to the Shepherd they need,
ready to follow his lead.
Angels have pointed the way,
now they are kneeling to pray.
Sleep, little Child, do not fear:
Mary and Joseph are near.
So sleep, while you may!

Smile, for the wise men will bring
gold for the One who is King,
incense to worship a Child,
God with us here reconciled,
myrrh for the Lord who will die,
rising to reign in the sky.
Sleep, little Child, do not fear:
Abba, your Father, is near.
So sleep, while you may!

Text: James Quinn, SJ, ©.
Possible Tune: POLISH CAROL
Topics: Christmas

Text: James Quinn, SJ, 1988, ©.
Possible Tune: WIEGENLIED
Topics: Christmas

Son of the Father,
Born Before Time's Dawn
10 10

Son of the Father, born before time's dawn,
rise as our Daystar, hope of all the world.

O Star of Jacob, light of heav'n above,
light up our darkness, shine upon us all.

Kings, kneel in homage; give to Christ, your King,
gold, myrrh, and incense, faith and hope and love.

This day God's glory dawns on Zion's hill;
now shall all nations walk in Zion's light.

Word of God,
from Mary's Womb
78 78 88

Word of God, from Mary's womb,
born to die for our salvation,
laid to rest within the tomb,
risen Lord of all creation:
bread of life, with new life feed us,
bread from heav'n, to heaven lead us.

Shepherd-King, for us you bled,
guard your sheep in love's safe keeping;
welcome home your faithful dead,
where no sound is heard of weeping:
Loving Shepherd, walk beside them,
through death's darkness safely guide them.

Living Lord, you conquered death,
come and take away our sadness;
breathe on us the Spirit's breath,
give us hope of heaven's gladness:
word of peace, all sorrow healing,
speak, your Father's love revealing.

Text: James Quinn, SJ, ©.
Possible Tune: GARDEN
Scripture References: st. 2: Num. 24:17; st.3: Matthew
    2:11; st. 4: Isaiah 2:2-5
Topics: Christmas, Epiphany, Life of Christ, King
    (Christ As)

Text: James Quinn, SJ, ©.
Possible Tune: LIEBSTER JESU
Topics: Funerals, Life of Christ, Word of God

Lord Jesus, from Your Wounded Side

87

Lord Jesus, from your wounded side
flowed out blood and water.

Lord Jesus, from your loving heart
well up living waters.

Lord Jesus, from your sacred heart
show us love and mercy.

Lord Jesus, Once on Tabor's Height

LMD

Lord Jesus, once on Tabor's height
you showed your glory as God's Son,
that glory which you laid aside
until your work on earth was done.
There Peter, James, and John are taught
that self-abasement shows God's power:
the hand of God will be revealed
in crucifixion's darkest hour.

With Moses and Elijah stands
a greater Law, a greater Word,
for Law and Prophets are fulfilled
as God the Father's voice is heard.
They speak with you about God's plan:
an Exodus of greater worth,
a greater Pasch, a world renewed,
in which the Church is brought to birth.

You teach us still how we must live
if we would share your great reward:
we must embrace your Cross of pain
to rise with you, our risen Lord.
Let all creation praise our God:
the Father, his beloved Son,
their Holy Spirit, Dove of peace,
Three Persons, yet for ever One.

Text: *Cor Jesu sacratissimum*;
    trans. by James Quinn, SJ, ©.
Topics: Blood of Christ, Mercy, Sacred Heart

Text: James Quinn, SJ, 1991, ©.
Possible Tune: ST. PATRICK
Topics: Cross of Christ, Transfiguration

Christ's Banner Guides Us on Christ's Way
LM

Christ's banner guides us on Christ's way,
the royal way of him who died!
O wondrous Cross, from which began
our life when Life was crucified!

Within Christ's heart, till heart should break,
the fount of life and love lay sealed;
by soldier's lance the living streams
of blood and water were revealed!

Then was fulfilled that word of old
which David once of Christ did sing,
that God in every land would reign!
Christ crucified is Lord and King!

O Cross, with noblest blood adorned,
the scarlet throne of royal grace,
we do you honor, for you bore
the Savior-King of Adam's race!

Upon your arms, in equal scales,
salvation's price was duly weighed;
the sinless One, for us made sin,
in sacrifice our ransom paid!

O Cross of Christ, in you we hope!
By you did Christ his victory win!
O holy Cross, our love increase,
in us destroy all power of sin!

All praise, O blessed Trinity,
be yours, from whom all graces flow!
On those who triumphed through the Cross
the victor's crown in heaven bestow!

Text: *Vexilla regis*, Venatius Fortunatus (c. 530-609);
    trans. by James Quinn, SJ, ©.
Possible Tune: BABYLON'S STREAMS
Topics: Cross, Holy Week, Lent, Opening of Worship,
    Processional

Spare Us, Spare Us, Lord
Irregular

Spare us, spare us, Lord,
be not angry for ever;
grant us forgiveness,
turn again and save us.

Text: James Quinn, SJ, ©.
Possible Tune: PARCE, DOMINE
Topics: Forgiveness, Lent, Penitence

May Glory, Praise, and Honor
76 76D

May glory, praise, and honor
be yours, O Savior King,
whose homage of Hosannas
from children's lips did spring!
You are the King of Zion,
King David's glorious Son,
who in God's name are coming,
O ever-blessed One!

The hosts of heaven praise you
in unison on high;
all peoples, all creation
in harmony reply!
Your chosen people met you,
each with a branch of palm;
now we, your People, greet you
with praise and prayer and psalm!

Before your bitter Passion
they offered you their praise;
now to your throne of glory
our hearts in song we raise!
Their praises then did please you;
so may the love we bring!
in all good is your pleasure,
O good and gracious King!

Refrain after last stanza
    May glory, praise, and honor
    be yours, O Savior King,
    whose homage of Hosannas
    from children's lips did spring!

Text: *Gloris, laus et honor*, St. Theodulph of Orleans
    (d. 821); trans. by James Quinn, SJ, ©.
Possible Tune: ST. THEODULPH
Topics: Lent, Palm Sunday

Now Let Us All with One Accord
LM

Now let us all with one accord,
in company with ages past,
keep vigil with our heav'nly Lord
in his temptation and his fast.

The covenant, so long revealed
to those of faith in former time,
Christ by his own example sealed
the Lord of love, in love sublime.

Your love, O Lord, our sinful race
has not returned, but falsified;
Author of mercy, turn your face
and grant repentance for our pride.

Remember, Lord, though frail we be,
in your own image were we made;
help us, lest in anxiety,
we cause your Name to be betrayed.

Therefore, we pray you, Lord, forgive;
so when our wand'rings here shall cease,
we may with you for ever live,
in love and unity and peace.

Lord Jesus, at This Hour You Took
LM

Lord Jesus, at this hour you took
the cross on which you conquered death;
you took the way that led to life,
the Spirit's gift your dying breath.

Almighty Father, at this hour
you sent the Spirit of your Son
to bring true peace to all on earth,
and make your scattered children one.

God's promised Gift, you came to warm
our lukewarm hearts with living fire;
bring now to life a lifeless world,
and loveless hearts with love inspire.

Praise God the Father, gracious Lord,
praise God his dear and only Son,
praise God the Spirit, bond of love,
praise God, who is for ever one.

Text: Attr. to Gregory the Great (540-604);
    trans. by James Quinn, SJ, 1972
Possible Tune: BOURBON
Scripture References: Matthew 4:1-11, Mark 1:12-13,
    Luke 4:1-3
Topics: Compassion, Covenant, Holy Week, Lent,
    Love (of God), Prayer,

Text: James Quinn, SJ, ©.
Possible Tune: JESU NOSTRA REDEMPTIO
Topics: Good Friday

Christ Keeps His Promised Hour
66 84D

Christ keeps his promised hour
before the Paschal feast;
his heart on fire with love reveals
love's perfect sign:
now bread becomes his flesh,
and wine his precious blood;
he gives his all to make all one
in him, God's Vine.

Among the olive-trees
he kneels upon the ground,
his body wet with drops of blood
from anguished heart;
he asks his chosen friends
to watch and pray with him
as he endures his agony
in prayer apart.

The soldier's lance strikes home;
the heart of Christ is pierced,
and from its depths the streams of grace
find swift release:
in water and in blood
the love of God is seen
that frees the world from stain of sin
and is its peace.

Our eucharistic feast
enshrines his sacred heart,
where love and joy and peace abound,
the source of grace,
this is God's pledge of bliss
when faith will yield to sight,
and eyes at last will see unveiled
the Savior's face.

All glory be to God,
the Father of our Lord,
to God the Son, whose heart reveals
eternal love,
to God the Spirit blest,
who formed Christ's sacred heart
and spreads on earth the peace of God
as heav'n-sent Dove.

Text: James Quinn, SJ, 1988, ©.
Possible Tune: LEONI
Scripture References: st. 1: John 13:1, John 2:1-11,
    Luke 22:14-20, John 15:1-8; st. 2: Luke 22:39-46;
    st. 3: John 19:34; st. 5: John 1:32-34
Topics: Cross of Christ, Good Friday, Life of Christ,
    Suffering of Christ

At This Same Hour, Redeemer King
LM

At this same hour, Redeemer King,
you climbed the cross, your royal throne;
your arms embracing heav'n and earth,
you claimed creation as your own.

This was your hour of trial, Lord,
when powers of darkness ruled the skies,
the darkest hour before the dawn
of endless day in Paradise.

This is the hour when courage flags,
when hearts grow faint and bodies tire;
come, Holy Spirit, flame of love,
to warm our hearts with love's own fire.

Praise God the Father, fount of grace;
praise God the Son, who set us free;
praise God the Spirit, Lord of life;
praise God the Blessed Trinity.

Forgive Them, Father Dear
SM

Forgive them, Father dear;
they know not what they do.
forgive all those who for my sake
forgive as I forgive.

This day redemption dawns,
the world begins anew.
This day you will enjoy with me
the peace of paradise.

O Woman, sinless Eve,
behold your newborn son.
O first to claim her as your own,
behold your Mother dear.

I cry to you, my God:
why have you left my side?
Yet you will be with me at last
when vict'ry will be mine.

I thirst with those who thirst
for living streams of grace.
I long to lead my thirsting sheep
to springs of endless life.

My task is now fulfilled;
my Father's work is done.
The Son may now retire to rest
within his Father's home.

Dear Father, I commend
my spirit to your care.
With this last prayer at eventide
I sleep in perfect peace.

Text: James Quinn, SJ, ©.
Source: *The seven words from the Cross*
Possible Tune: SAEVO DOLORUM TURBINE
Scripture References: st. 4: Matthew 27:46 Psalm 22:1
Topics: Evening, Forgiveness, Good Friday, Lent,
    Stations of the Cross

Text: James Quinn, SJ, ©.
Possible Tune: DEUS, TUORUM MILITUM
Topics: Cross of Christ, Good Friday, Prayer, Suffering
    of Christ

Jesus on the Cross Is Lying
887 D

Jesus on the cross is dying;
soon his body will be lying
in the darkness of the tomb.

God's own Mother, purest maiden,
sees the sinless One sin-laden,
blessed fruit of blessed womb.

Mary's heart for him is aching
as she sees her Son's heart breaking
so that love may be revealed.

Now at last her heart is feeling
sorrow's sword, her Son revealing
thoughts in many hearts concealed.

How could pity not awaken
for the Son of God, forsaken
in the loneliness of death?

Who would not give consolation
in this Mother's desolation
as he breathes his dying breath?

Mary's heart for him is bleeding;
in his blood. for sinners pleading,
God's new law of love is sealed.

"It is done," she hears him crying
at the moment of his dying:
death by death has now been healed.

Mary, Mother of compassion,
let me share with you his passion:
grant me now this grace of grace.

Let my heart with love be burning
for my wounded Jesus, yearning
for the vision of his face.

Queen of martyrs, Virgin-Mother,
sorrow-laden as no other,
let me share your agony.

Let me stand beside you, sharing
grief for Jesus, my sins bearing
on the cross of Calvary.

Share with me your tears of sadness,
make his passion all my gladness,
Mary, Mother of my Lord.

By the cross your vigil keeping,
let me share your silent weeping,
pierce my heart with sorrow's sword.

Mother, turn to me in blessing,
let me live, your grief expressing,
all my days upon this earth.

Let me, though in humble fashion,
share with you the bitter passion
of the Son you brought to birth.

Let me bear the wounds of Jesus,
drink the precious blood that frees us,
glory only in his cross.

At the judgment interceding,
stand by me, with Jesus pleading,
save me from eternal loss.

Let the cross be my salvation,
Jesus' death my consolation,
in that hour when I must die.

Queen of heaven, by the merit
of your Son let me inherit
joy with all the saints on high.
Amen.

Text: *Stabat mater dolorosa,* 13th cent.; trans. by
James Quinn, SJ, ©.
Possible Tune: STABAT MATER
Topics: Good Friday, Lent, Mary, Stations of the Cross

Judge of the World,
You Are Judged Unjustly
Stations of the Cross
10 8 with refrain

Judge of the world, you are judged unjustly:
Lord of all, be my Savior-King.
Refrain
Let me know in my heart the pain of your Passion,
King of Glory, my only love.

Passover Lamb, you are led to slaughter:
Lord, your cross is my hope and joy. *Refrain*

Healer of all, now your footsteps falter:
Jesus, Lord, make me strong in faith. *Refrain*

Eyes of your Mother meet yours in pity:
Son of Mary, reward her tears. *Refrain*

Stranger now shoulders a stranger's burden:
God of grief, you have shouldered mine. *Refrain*

Bloodstained and bruised is your face, my Jesus:
Son of God, look with love on me. *Refrain*

Seeking the fallen, you fall exhausted:
Jesus, Lord, may I rise from sin. *Refrain*

Here is the shadow of coming judgment:
Lord, forgive me for all my sins. *Refrain*

Stumbling, you share in our mortal weakness:
Jesus, Lord, make my spirit strong. *Refrain*

Maker of all, you are left with nothing:
losing all, you enrich us, Lord. *Refrain*

Open your arms to embrace creation:
nail me, Lord, to the cross with you. *Refrain*

Into God's hands you commend your spirit:
dying Lord, may I die for you. *Refrain*

Tenderly Mary receives your body:
body broken, you are my strength. *Refrain*

Silent, you wait for your Easter glory:
buried Lord, make me rise with you. *Refrain*

Text: James Quinn, SJ, ©.
Possible Tune: CAOINEADH NA MAIGHDINE (Trad. Irish)
Topics: Stations of the Cross

The New Eve Stands Before the Tree
LM

The new Eve stands before the Tree,
the sinless Mother of our race;
this is the hour when Adam gives
at Eve's request the wine of grace.

It is achieved: redemption dawns;
though skies are dark, yet hope is bright;
your death, Lord Jesus, is our life,
your grave the womb of radiant light.

To God your Father you commit
your spirit, Lord, in perfect love;
to you in turn he will entrust
the Holy Spirit, gentle Dove.

Praise God the Father, Lord of all,
praise God the Son, our victory,
praise God the Spirit of their love,
praise God, one God, eternally.

The New Eve Stands Before the Tree (II)
LM

The new Eve stands before the Tree;
her dying Son speaks words of love:
he gives his Mother as our Queen
on earth below, in heav'n above.

The second Adam sleeps in death,
his side is pierced, his heart unsealed;
the grace-filled Church, his sinless Bride,
in blood and water is revealed.

We thank you, Father, for the Church,
where Christ is King and Mary Queen,
where through your Spirit you unfold
a world of glory yet unseen.

Text: James Quinn, SJ, ©.
Possible Tune: O AMOR QUAM ECSTATICUS
Topics: Good Friday, Lent, Mary

Text: James Quinn, SJ, 1993
Scripture References: John 19:26-27, 34;
Genesis 2:21-24; Ephesians 5:25-27.
Topics: Good Friday, Mary

Christ Is Victor

Christ is Victor!
Christ is Ruler!
Christ the King is Lord of all!

Text: *Christus vincit,* 8th to 9th cent., trans. by James
    Quinn, SJ, ©.
Possible Tune: CHRISTUS VINCIT
Topics: Communion, Easter

Now to the Throne
of God in Exultation
11 10 11 10

Now to the throne of God in exultation,
angels of heav'n, your proud Hosannas sing!
Trumpets on high, salute God's new creation,
waking the day to greet its Lord and King!

Now let the earth be filled with songs of gladness:
Christ is our Dawn, and banished is our night!
Now let the world acclaim the King of ages,
rising as Lord of everlasting light!

Sing in your joy, O holy Church, our Mother:
darkest of nights becomes your day of days!
Now, in the dawn of never-ending glory,
bring to your Lord the homage of your praise!

Bless with your love this feast of light, O Father!
Shine on the world, O world's true Light, God's
Son!
Touch with your fire, O God the Holy Spirit,
tongues to proclaim the triumph Christ has won!

Text: *Exultet;* trans. by James Quinn, SJ, ©.
Possible Tune: EASTWOOD
Topics: Easter, Easter Vigil, Praise, Resurrection,
    Victory

Christ Was of Old,
Yet Christ Is of Today
10 10 10 10

Christ was of old, yet Christ is of today;
timeless he lives in everlasting day.
He is the Lord on whom all things depend,
their one Beginning and their only End.

Christ is the Alpha, Fount of all that is,
the End, the Omega, for all is his.
He rules all time, each age and every hour;
to him belong all eternal praise and power.

Christ by his glorious wounds in safety keep
his little flock, true Shepherd of his sheep.
May he who rose to glory from death's night
shine on our hearts and minds with Easter light.

Text: *Christus heri et hodie* (Easter Vigil); trans. by
    James Quinn, SJ, ©.
Possible Tune: JULIUS
Topics: Easter, Easter Vigil, Life of Christ

Easter Glory Fills the Sky!

77 77 with alleluias

Easter glory fills the sky!	Alleluia!
Christ now lives, no more to die!	Alleluia!
Darkness has been put to flight	Alleluia!
by the living Lord of light!	Alleluia!

See the stone is rolled away	Alleluia!
from the tomb where once he lay!	Alleluia!
He has risen as he said,	Alleluia!
glorious Firstborn from the dead!	Alleluia!

Mary, Mother, greet your Son,	Alleluia!
radiant from his triumph won!	Alleluia!
By his cross you shared his pain,	Alleluia!
so for ever share his reign!	Alleluia!

Magd'len, wipe away your tears!	Alleluia!
he has come who calms your fears!	Alleluia!
Hear the Master speak your name;	Alleluia!
turn to him with heart aflame!	Alleluia!

Shepherd, seek the sheep that strayed!	Alleluia!
Come to contrite Peter's aid!	Alleluia!
Strengthen him to be the rock;	Alleluia!
make him shepherd of your flock!	Alleluia!

Seek not life within the tomb;	Alleluia!
Christ stands in the upper room!	Alleluia!
Risen glory he conceals,	Alleluia!
risen Body he reveals!	Alleluia!

Though we see his face no more,	Alleluia!
he is with us as before!	Alleluia!
Glory veiled, he is our Priest,	Alleluia!
his true flesh and blood our feast!	Alleluia!

Christ, the Victor over death,	Alleluia!
breathes on us the Spirit's breath!	Alleluia!
Paradise is our reward,	Alleluia!
endless Easter with our Lord!	Alleluia!

Our Gospel Is the Risen Christ

CM

Our Gospel is the risen Christ:
   how can the dead not rise?
If none who dies will rise again,
   Christ died to rise no more.

If Christ still lies within the tomb,
   our Gospel is in vain,
your faith is folly, sin remains,
   dead are the dead in Christ.

If hope in Christ is for this life,
   and for this life alone,
then pity us, whose hope will die:
   we need your pity most.

But Christ in truth has ris'n again,
   firstfruits of all the dead;
as from one man came death to all,
   so from one man came life.

As all in Adam come to die,
   so all in Christ will live;
Christ rose the first, then those in Christ
   will rise at his return.

Then will the consummation be:
   his Kingdom Christ will give
yo God the Father, conquered now
   all kingship, rule, and power.

Christ will be King till Christ has laid
   all foes beneath his feet,
when he will pass the doom of death
   on Death, the final foe.

When all is giv'n to God's own Son,
   then he himself will give
all that he has to God, who gave,
   who will be all in all.

Text: James Quinn, SJ, ©.
Possible Tune: GWALCHMAI or FRANCOIS
Topics: Alleluias, Easter, Resurrection

Text: James Quinn, SJ, ©.
Possible Tune: MARTYRS
Scripture Reference: 1 Corinthians 15:12-28
Topics: Easter, Funerals, King (Christ As)

O Flock of Christ, Your Homage Bring

88 8 with alleluias

O Flock of Christ, your homage bring
to Christ the Lamb, your glorious King!
His Easter praise in triumph sing!
    Alleluia, alleluia, alleluia!

Peace has come down from God on high!
The King of peace in death did lie!
To save the sheep the Lamb did die!

Never on earth was stranger sight:
life fought with death in darkest night,
yet lives to reign in endless light!

What saw you, Mary, on your way?
"'I saw the tomb where Life once lay,
whose glory shone this Easter Day!

"Angels their joyful tidings spread!
Grave-clothes I saw where none lay dead,
the cloth that once had veiled his head!

"Christ is my hope, who rose for me!
Soon will you all his glory see!
Christ bids you go to Galilee!"

Christ lives again, whose blood was shed,
the Lord of life, our living Bread,
the Firstborn risen from the dead!
    Alleluia, alleluia, alleluia!

Text: *Victimae paschali*, 11th cent.; trans. by James
    Quinn, SJ, ©.
Possible Tune: VULPIUS (GELOBT SEI GOTT)
Topics: Alleluias, Easter

Praise Him As He Mounts the Skies

77 77 with alleluias

Praise him as he mounts the skies,   Alleluia!
Christ, the Lord of Paradise!   Alleluia!
Cry hosanna in the height   Alleluia!
as he rises out of sight!   Alleluia!

Now at last he takes his throne,   Alleluia!
from all ages his alone!   Alleluia!
With his praise creation rings: Alleluia!
"Lord of lords and King of kings!"   Alleluia!

Hands and feet and side reveal   Alleluia!
wounds of love, high priesthood's seal!   Alleluia!
Advocate, for us he pleads;   Alleluia!
Heavenly Priest, he intercedes!   Alleluia!

Christians, raise your eyes above!   Alleluia!
He will come again in love,   Alleluia!
on that great and wondrous day   Alleluia!
when this world will pass away!   Alleluia!

At his word new heavens and earth   Alleluia!
will in glory spring to birth!   Alleluia!
Risen Lord, our great Amen,   Alleluia!
come, Lord Jesus, come again!   Alleluia!

Text: James Quinn, SJ, ©.
Possible Tune: LLANFAIR, FENTON (Urwin)
Scripture References: st. 3: Hebrews 7:24-25, 8:1-3;
    st. 4-5: Isaiah 65:17-18; II Corinthians 1:20, II Peter
    3:11-13, Revelations 22:20
Topics: Alleluias, Ascension and Reign, Creation, King
    (Christ as), New Heaven and Earth, Praise

Now, from the Heav'ns Descending

76 76D

Now, from the heav'ns descending,
is seen a glorious light,
the Bride of Christ in splendor,
arrayed in purest white.
She is the Holy City,
whose radiance is the grace
of all the saints in glory,
from every time and place.

This is the hour of gladness
for Bridegroom and for Bride;
the Lamb's great feast is ready;
his Bride is at his side.
How bless'd are those invited
to share his wedding-feast:
the least become the greatest,
the greatest are the least.

He who is throned in heaven
takes up his dwelling-place
among his chosen people
who see him face to face.
No sound is heard of weeping,
for pain and sorrow cease,
and sin shall reign no longer,
but love and joy and peace.

See how a new creation
is brought at last to birth,
a new and glorious heaven,
a new and glorious earth.
Death's power for ever broken,
its empire swept away,
the promised dawn of glory
begins its endless day.

Text: James Quinn, SJ, ©.
Possible Tune: AURELIA, NOVILLE
Scripture References: Rev. 19:6-9, 21:1-5
Topics: Ascension and Reign, Church, Funerals,
    New Heaven

Around the Throne of God I Heard

LM

Around the throne of God I heard
the heav'ns with angel voices ring;
from myriad choirs that sang his praise
I heard the song that angels sing:

"To Christ, the Lamb that once was slain,
all kingship, riches, wisdom, might,
all honor, glory, blessing be,
for all is his by sov'reign right."

All living things in heav'n above,
all living things of earth and sea,
took up the song the angels sang,
and echoed back their minstrelsy:

"All blessing, honor, glory, power
for evermore to God be giv'n,
and equal praise to Christ the Lamb,
enthroned with him in highest heav'n."

So now with angels round the throne,
with every living creature, raise
to God and God's victorious Lamb
the Alleluia of your praise.

Text: James Quinn, SJ, ©.
Possible Tune: CHURCH TRIUMPHANT
Scripture Reference: Rev. 5:11-13
Topics: Angels, Easter, New Heaven and Earth, Praise

Holy Spirit, Lord, Gift of God
888 6

Holy Spirit, Lord, Gift of God,
Holy Spirit, Lord, light of truth,
Holy Spirit, Lord, fire of love,
   come, Holy Spirit, come.

Holy Spirit, Lord, Breath of God,
Holy Spirit, Lord, Breath of life,
Holy Spirit, Lord, mighty wind,
   come, Holy Spirit, come.

Holy Spirit, Lord, living flame,
Holy Spirit, Lord, cleansing fire,
Holy Spirit, Lord, burning light,
   come, Holy Spirit, come.

Holy Spirit, Lord, give us faith,
Holy Spirit, Lord, give us hope,
Holy Spirit, Lord, give us love,
   come, Holy Spirit, come.

Holy Spirit, Lord, come in love,
Holy Spirit, Lord, come in joy,
Holy Spirit, Lord, come in peace,
   come, Holy Spirit, come.

Holy Spirit, Lord, set us free,
Holy Spirit, Lord, keep us true,
Holy Spirit, Lord, make us one,
   come, Holy Spirit, come.

Holy Spirit from on High
777D

Holy Spirit from on high,
shine upon our inward eye,
   pierce the blindness of our sight!
Come, Befriender, to our aid;
come with gifts that never fade;
   come and bathe us in your light!

Come, Consoler Spirit blest,
troubled soul's most welcome Guest,
   healing hand that brings relief,
restful ease in toil and stress,
cooling wind when heats oppress,
   calm and comfort in our grief.

Light of lights, in darkness shine,
flood our hearts with light divine,
   burn within is, living Fire!
Go before us; guide our way,
for without you we must stray:
   sinful hearts with grace inspire!

What is stained by sin, renew;
what is dry, with grace bedew;
   strength to wounded souls restore!
Coldness with your ardor burn;
willfulness to wisdom turn;
   crooked ways make straight once more!

To your people come in love;
all our hope is from above;
   with your sevenfold grace descend!
Come with virtue's high reward;
come in death as living Lord;
   come with joy that knows no end!

Text: James Quinn, SJ, 1989, ©.
Topics: Confirmation, Holy Spirit, Pentecost

Text: *Veni, sancte spiritus*, 13th cent., trans. by James
   Quinn, SJ, ©.
Possible Tune: VENI, SANCTE
Topics: Confirmation, Holy Spirit, Pentecost

Come, Holy Spirit, Fire of Truth
88 87

Come, Holy Spirit, fire of truth,
to share with us your heav'nly light;
enrich our minds, inflame our hearts
with your resplendent vision.

Come, Holy Spirit, bond of love,
to make our lukewarm hearts your own;
forgive our sins, renew our zeal,
and dwell in us for ever.

Come, Holy Spirit, as of old
you gave to Mary God's own Son,
so make God's children like her Child,
belov'd of God our Father.

Come, Holy Spirit, Lord of life,
come, lead us home to heaven's joy,
to see the Father with his Son
in you, their Holy Spirit.

Father, Lord of Earth and Heaven
CM

Father Lord of earth and heaven,
King to whom all gifts belong,
give your greatest Gift, your Spirit,
God the holy, God the strong.

Son of God, enthroned in glory,
send your promised Gift of grace,
make your Church your holy Temple,
God the Spirit's dwelling-place.

Spirit, come, in peace descending
as at Jordan, heav'nly Dove,
seal your Church as God's anointed,
set our hearts on fire with love.

Stay among us, God the Father,
stay among us, God the Son,
stay among us, Holy Spirit:
dwell within us, make us one.

Text: James Quinn, SJ, 1991, ©.
Possible Tune: SANCTI VENITE
Topics: Holy Spirit, Pentecost

Text: James Quinn, SJ, ©.
Possible Tune: SUSSEX
Topics: Confirmation, Maundy Thursday, Pentecost

Jesus, Your Church Was Built on Firm Foundations

11 11 11 5

Jesus, your Church was built on firm foundations,
resting securely on the Twelve Apostles!
Still stands their college, lasting through all ages!
Wise was your building!

Jesus, true God and Rock of our salvation!
Yours is the title that you gave to Simon,
naming him Peter as the Church's bedrock,
first of apostles!

Jesus, sole Ruler in the Church, your kingdom,
yours are the keys that open David's city!
Yet till your coming Peter is your viceroy,
keys in his keeping!

Jesus, our Lover, watchful for our safety,
love was the test you gave to your chief shepherd,
love for yourself and for the flock you cherish,
Shepherd most loving!

Jesus, we thank you for the Church, your Body!
Keep us all one with you and with each other,
one with our bishop, one with your chief shepherd,
Peter's successor!

Jesus, good Shepherd, you have died to save us!
Make one in love all those who call you Savior!
May there be soon one loving flock, one sheepfold,
one blest communion.

Creator Spirit, Lord of Grace

LM

Creator Spirit, Lord of grace,
come, make in us your dwelling-place!
O purest Light, in darkness shine;
fill loveless hearts, O Love divine!

Befriender, hear your people's cry!
Come down, O Gift of God most high!
Descend in peace, O heav'nly Dove;
come, fount of life; come, flame of love!

As once on Christ the Servant's head
the oil of sevenfold grace you shed,
so now anoint from love's deep springs
your chosen prophets, priests, and kings!

Of every gift the living source,
of mighty deeds the unseen force,
the Father sends his promised One
to speak for all who serve his Son!

Keep far all those who wish us ill!
O Dove of peace, be with us still!
In every danger at our side,
O Friend, befriend us; be our guide!

Reveal to us the Father's love,
reveal his Son, who reigns above!
To truth, O Truth, our minds make true;
in love, O Love, our hearts renew!

Text: James Quinn, SJ, ©.
Possible Tune: ISTE CONFESSOR
Topics: Apostles, Church, Easter

Text: *Veni, creator spiritus*, 8th or 9th cent., trans. by
    James Quinn, SJ, ©.
Possible Tune: ROCKINGHAM
Topics: Confirmation, Holy Spirit, Pentecost

God All-Holy, Fountain of Life
LM

God all-holy, fountain of life,
King of the ages, Lord of all,
God of compassion, God of grace,
loving Father, gaze on your Son.

Word and Wisdom, light of the world,
priest of creation, living Bread,
firstborn in glory, Lamb of God,
Son of Mary, grant us your peace.

Holy Spirit, fire of God's love,
promise of heaven, gift of God,
comfort in sorrow, dove of peace,
yoy unending, dwell in our hearts.

Sing, creation, sing to the Lord:
glory and honor be to God,
one in three Persons, one in love,
now and always, world without end.

Text: James Quinn, SJ, ©.
Possible Tunes: DEUS MEUS, ADIUVA ME
Topics: Music, Trinity

Biblical Songs

Give Answer, O God of Grace
Psalm 4
12 12 12 12

Give answer, O God of grace, give heed to my prayer.
From trouble you rescued me, have pity and hear.
O hearts full of pride, how long will you stay unmoved?
How long will you seek and love the vain and the false?

The Lord is a gracious God to all whom he loves.
The Lord bends his ear to me whenever I call.
Fear not, do not sin: at night praise God and be still.
Make goodness your gift to God; have trust in the Lord.

How many abandon hope of joy that will last!
My God, may your face shine forth with joy for my heart.
You give to my heart, O Lord, true joy unalloyed.
No harvest of wheat or vine brings joy such as yours.

I lie down to rest, and sleep enfolds me in peace,
For you are my fortress, Lord, in you I am safe.
Give thanks to the God of grace; give thanks to his Son,
give thanks to the bond of peace, the Spirit of love.

Text: Psalm 4, para. by James Quinn, SJ, 1990, ©.
Possible Tune: THE SONG OF THE SEA
Topics: Comfort, Evening, Guidance

Great Is Your Glory, O God
Psalm 8
12 13 12 13

Great is your glory, O God, throughout all the world!
Bright hosts of high heav'n fill the air with hymns to your name,
while children and babes by their songs make perfect your praise!
Your high tower in heaven stands firm, and foiled are your foes!

Wonder is mine as I gaze on heaven above!
Your fingers have fixed in the sky, the moon, and the stars!
You still spare a thought for mankind! O marvel of man!
Frail man that is destined to die your mercy enfolds!

Made in your likeness is man, an angel on earth!
His glory of grace is your gift, rich crown for his head!
High king you enthroned him on earth, the Lord of the world!
Creation you gave to be his, to master and own!

All has been given to man: the oxen, the sheep,
the beasts that roam wild on the earth, in mountain or plain,
the birds that fly free through the air, the fish of the sea!
How great is your glory, O God, throughout all the world!

My Shepherd Is My Lord and God
Psalm 23 (22)
87 87

My Shepherd is my Lord and God:
I shall not want for ever.
He sets me down to take my ease
in fresh and tender meadows.

He leads me out by peaceful streams
of cool, refreshing waters.
He guides me right by chosen paths:
he is my faithful Shepherd.

In darkness I shall know no fear,
for you are by me always.
I look to Shepherd's crook and staff
to comfort and protect me.

For me you have prepared a feast
where all my foes can see me.
You pour your oil upon my head;
my cup is brimming over.

Your love and kindness will be mine
through all the days that follow.
The house of God shall be my home
for ever and for ever.

Text: Psalm 23 (22), para. by James
Quinn, SJ, ©.
Possible Tune: DOMINUS REGIT ME
Topics: Comfort, Communion, Funerals,
Shepherd

Text: Psalm 8, para. by James Quinn, SJ, ©.
Possible Tune: SLAN BEO
Topics: Creation, Praise

Loving Shepherd, King Divine
Psalm 23 (22)
77 77

Loving Shepherd, King divine,
I have all since you are mine.
I shall know not want or care;
when I need you, you are there.

Shepherd, you will guide my feet
by cool meadows in the heat.
You will find in deserts drear
peaceful pools to give me cheer.

Lead me by your chosen way;
never let me from you stray.
My good Shepherd you will be;
never will you part from me.

In the darkness you are near;
you will take away my fear.
In all troubles I will look
to my Shepherd's staff and crook.

Oil of gladness on my head,
now I share the feast you spread.
Now my cup of joy o'erflows
in the sight of all my foes.

Love and kindness you will show
everywhere that I may go.
In your household I will rest
evermore as your loved guest.

You Are My Shepherd, Lord
Psalm 23 (22)
66 66 with refrain

You are my shepherd, Lord,
you lead me to pasture.
All that I want or need
your goodness will give me.
    Refrain
        Lead us in paths of peace,
        our King and our Shepherd.

Shepherd, you set me down
in grass cool and tender,
watered by living streams,
refreshing my spirit. *Refrain*

Sure are your Shepherd's ways
by which you will guide me.
Even in darkest night
no fear will disturb me. *Refrain*

Lord, you are always near;
your presence protects me.
Shepherd, your crook and staff
give comfort and courage. *Refrain*

Lord, in the sight of all
I sit at your table.
Oil of your joy you pour,
my cup fills with gladness. *Refrain*

Shepherd, your steadfast love
will follow me always.
So shall I share your home
for ever and ever. *Refrain*

Text: Psalm 23 (22), para. by James Quinn, SJ, ©.
Possible Tune: BUCKLAND
Scripture Reference: Psalm 23
Topics: Christian Life, Comfort, Communion, Funerals,
    Guidance, Shepherd

Text: Psalm 23 (22) para. by James Quinn, SJ, ©.
Possible Tune: PSALM 23 (O'Hanlon)
Topics: Christian Life, Comfort, Guidance, Shepherd

To Those Who Revere You, O Lord
Psalm 25 (24)
LM

To those who revere you, O Lord,
you point out the way to your love,
the path to your promise of bliss:
their children inherit the land.

The upright, O Lord, you befriend,
revealing your law in their hearts.
My eyes are on you every hour,
you rescue my feet from the snare.

Lord, look on your servant with love,
on one who is friendless, alone.
Give ease to the pain in my heart,
give comfort in all my distress.

My burden is heavy to bear:
remove all my sins from your sight.
You see how my foes crowd around,
how fierce is the hate in their eyes.

Lord, come to me, rescue my soul:
my refuge, I trust in your power.
Your goodness and justice I know:
my hope, Lord, is only in you.

The Father of mercies be blessed,
the Son of his love be acclaimed,
their Spirit of wisdom be praised,
one God be for ever adored.

Response
I bless you by day and by night,
I bless you in sickness and health,
for you are my Lord and my God,
the God who forgives and who saves.

To You, Lord, I Lift Up My Heart
Psalm 25 (24)
LM

To you, Lord, I lift up my heart,
in you, Lord, I place all my trust.
Lord, let nor my hope be in vain,
no enemy laugh me to scorn.

All those who have faith in your word
will never have cause to be shamed,
but those who break faith with your love
will reap the reward of their sin.

Lord, teach me the way of your truth,
Lord, teach me the path of your love,
Lord, guide me to find you in peace,
my teacher, my Savior, my God.

You, Lord, are for ever my hope,
because you are faithful and true.
Remember your mercy, my God,
your love that is steadfast and sure.

Forget, Lord, the sins of my youth,
remember me always with love,
for you have compassion on all,
you search for all those who have strayed.

The gentle you guide in your ways,
you show the right path to the meek,
your ways, Lord, are loving and kind
with those who are true to your law.

With trust I now call on your name:
your love will forgive me my sins,
which lie like a weight on my heart,
which now I confess in your sight.

Text: Psalm 25 (24), para. by James Quinn, SJ, ©.
Topics: Comfort and Encouragement, Refuge

Text: Psalm 25 (24), para. by James Quinn, SJ, ©.
Topics: Christian Life, Guidance, Hope

God Is My Light, My Life
Psalm 27 (26)
66 66 with refrain

Refrain
Christ is my faith, my hope,
my love everlasting.

God is my light, my life,
what fear can disturb me?
God is my sure defense,
what power can defeat me?
    Refrain

This is my heart's desire,
to dwell in God's presence,
always to see his face,
and savor his goodness.
    Refrain

Lord, it is you I seek,
your vision my longing;
turn not away your face,
for you are my helper.
    Refrain

Now is my heart at rest:
I trust in his goodness;
wait for the Lord in hope,
in him put your courage.
    Refrain

I Will Thank the Lord in Joy and Sorrow
Psalm 34 (33)
10 8 10 8 with refrain (10 8)

Response
I will bless your goodness, God my Father;
you make me one with Christ, your Son.

I will thank the Lord in joy and sorrow,
my tongue shall always tell his praise;
in the Lord alone my spirit glories;
the sad at heart take heart anew.

Turn your face to God, and shine in splendor;
his presence drives away all fear;
when the poor cry out, the Lord is listening;
he rescues them in all their need.

Like an army, angels gather round us,
to shelter those who fear his name.
Taste and see how gracious is his goodness!
How happy those who trust in God!

Keep your tongue from speaking any evil,
your lips from any lying word;
turn aside from wrong to ways of goodness,
and always seek the paths of peace.

God will set his face against the wicked;
their name will fade beyond recall;
he will turn to hear his faithful servants,
and give them what they ask in love.

When they pray, the Lord will hear them calling,
and prove himself their friend in need;
he is near to heal the broken-hearted,
the downcast he uplifts in love.

Text: Psalm 27 (26):1,4, 8b-9c, 13-14;
    para. by James Quinn, SJ, ©.
Topics: Light, Love (God to us)

Text: Psalm 34 (33):2-3, 6-9, 14-19;
    para. by James Quinn, SJ, ©.
Topics: Christian Life, Comfort and Encouragement,
    Justice, Thanksgiving

My Soul Is Like the Deer
Psalm 42 (41)
66 66

My soul is like the deer
that longs for living streams.
What does my soul desire
but you, my living Lord?

I thirst for God on high,
the living God above:
when may I enter in
and see the face of God?

I weep by day and night;
my tears become my bread,
all day I hear them say:
where is your God and Lord?

I think of days gone by
as I pour out my soul:
God's people I would lead
into the house of God.

Around me they would sing
in joy and thankfulness;
boundless would be their joy
within God's holy house.

My soul, why are you sad?
Why do you moan and sigh?
In him still hope; still praise
your Savior and your God.

Praise the Almighty,
for All Praise Is Due to Him
Psalm 48 (47)
12 7 11 7 10 8 11 7

Praise the Almighty, for all praise is due to him,
Zion, well-beloved of God;
city of loveliness, throned on God's mountain,
Zion, joy of all the earth,
heart of the world and queen of creation,
palace of God, the mighty King,
dwelling within you is God the almighty,
Zion's pride and Zion's strength.

Lord, in your Temple we think on your graciousness,
love divine that knows no end;
wide as the world is the fame of your glory.
everlasting is your name;
full are your hands of love and of goodness,
making the heart of Zion glad;
wise are your counsels and just are your
    judgments,
righteous Judge and loving Lord.

Pilgrims to Zion, take pride in her citadel;
mark her might, her towers tall;
walk round her walls and behold how securely
Zion stands, whose strength is God;
tell Zion's sons the secret of Zion:
Zion is safe with God as guide;
Zion is strong when she trusts the Almighty,
Zion's God for evermore.

Text: Psalm 42:1-5 (41:2-6)
    para. by James Quinn, SJ, ©.
Possible Tune: ST. CECILIA
Topics: Easter Vigil, Hope

Text: Psalm 48 (47):1-3, 9-14;
    para. by James Quinn, SJ, ©.
Possible Tune: RIBHINN
Topics: Dedication, New Heaven and Earth, Praise

Have Pity, God of Grace, on Me, a Sinner
Psalm 51 (50)
11 10 11 10

Have pity, God of grace, on me, a sinner;
my sinful heart in your great love console.
Cleanse me, O fount of grace, from sin's
    defilement;
bathe me, O healing spring, and make me whole.

True hearts alone, O God of truth, delight you;
my heart of hearts to truth make ever true.
Give me a wiser heart to learn true wisdom;
by steadfast love my waywardness undo.

Let me, I pray, live always in your presence;
give me your Spirit, Lord, to guide me still.
Give me anew the joy of your salvation;
renew my spirit and uphold my will.

All glory be to God, the gracious Father,
all glory be to God, his only Son,
all glory be to God, the Holy Spirit,
who dwell in us by grace and make us one.

My Spirit is Thirsting
Psalm 63 (62)
68 68 with refrain

Response
Lord Jesus, remember
all those who have died in your peace.

My spirit is thirsting:
I long for the sight of my God.
My body is weary,
like land that is waiting for rain.

I come to your temple,
to see you in glory and power.
My tongue sings your praises:
to love you is greater than life.

I bless you for ever;
my hands are uplifted in prayer.
You fill me with blessings;
I thank you with joy in my heart.

You, Lord are my helper:
the shade of your wing is my joy.
I trust you in all things:
your right hand upholds me in strength.

Sing praise to the Father,
to Jesus, the Son of his love.
Sing praise to the Spirit,
one God with both Father and Son.

Text: James Quinn, SJ, based on Psalm 51 (50)
Possible Tune: INTERCESSOR
Topics: Forgiveness, Lent, Penitence, Sanctification

Text: Psalm 63 (62), para. by James Quinn, SJ, ©.
Topics: Gratitude, Joy, Praise and Adoration,
    Thanksgiving

Lovely Your Dwelling Is
Psalm 84 (83)
12 10 12 10

Lovely your dwelling is,
Lord, God of heav'nly hosts!
How I have longed to be
within your courts!
Heart, beat with love divine;
tongue, tell your tale of joy,
sing to the living God
your song of bliss!

Sparrow and swallow build
nests for their brood of young;
so by your altar-throne
in peace I rest!
Dwellers within your house
praise you in endless song,
happy to share as guests
your hearth and home!

Blessed are those who seek
strength from your strength alone;
happy the pilgrims set
on Zion's way!
Where desert valleys lie
pilgrims will find cool springs;
fruitful the land will be
from autumn rains!

Pilgrims to Zion's hill
strength upon strength will gain
till at their journey's end
your glory dawns!
Hear this our pilgrims' prayer:
still be our shield, O Lord,
bless your anointed one,
be Israel's God!

One day within your courts
is bliss of heav'n to me,
more than a thousand days
of worldly joy!
Let me but stand and knock,
waiting for entrance here;
poor I would rather be
than rich in sin!

God is my light and shield;
blessing he will bestow,
making his glory shine
on us, his friends!
No prayer will he refuse
pilgrims who tread his path;
happy the man who trusts
in you, O Lord!

Text: Psalm 84 (83), para. by James Quinn, SJ, ©.
Possible Tune: QUAM DILECTA
Topics: Church, Funerals, Heaven, Opening of Worship,
    Processional

I Listen to God
As He Tells Me
Psalm 85 (84)
95 95 with refrain

Response
The Lord is the giver of goodness,
the God of my peace.

I listen to God as he tells me
the word of his peace;
his voice speaks of peace for his people,
of peace for his friends.

His peace is on all who will seek him
in truth, in their hearts,
on sinners who turn from their sinning
to God in his love.

His help is at hand for his servants,
revering his name;
his presence will dwell in his Temple,
the glory of God.

His love is his blessing on goodness,
his peace on our truth;
his lips will bestow on our justice
the kiss of his peace.

The Lord will make Israel prosper,
our land yield its fruit,
when goodness will walk as his herald
with gifts of his peace.

On Zion's Mount
the City Stands
Psalm 87 (86)
CM

On Zion's mount the City stands,
beloved of the Lord,
God's dwelling-place in Israel,
the City of his throne.

Of you is glory prophesied,
O City of our God;
your glory God himself proclaims,
O City of his love:

"Among my friends shall Egypt be,
among them Babylon;
Philistia, Tyre, and Nubia's race
shall be each Zion's child."

Of all shall Zion Mother be,
each nation Zion's son.
This Mother-City God shall keep
secure for evermore.

God's scroll of nations shall record:
"This one is Zion's child."
All nations shall rejoice, and sing:
"In Zion is our home."

Text: Psalm 87 (86), para. by James Quinn, SJ, ©.
Possible Tune: ST. MAGNUS (NOTTINGHAM)
Topics: Church, New Heaven, Unity

Text: Psalm 85 (84):9-14, para. by James Quinn, SJ, ©.
Topics: Peace (Inner), Penitence

The Lord Is King, Enthroned on High
Psalm 93 (92)
CM

The Lord is King, enthroned on high
in might and majesty;
he sits arrayed in royal state,
in robes of sov'reign power.

He is the everlasting King,
who reigns eternally.
He made the world; he guides it still
with never-failing love.

The mighty ocean lifts its voice;
the surging sea gives tongue;
the thunder of the roaring waves
proclaims his wondrous power.

More glorious than the stormy sea,
more splendid than its calm
is God, our Lord, who reigns above,
eternal King of kings.

Your works reveal your wisdom, Lord,
in you our trust is firm;
for endless days shall Zion be
your holy house, O God.

To God the Father be all praise,
all glory be his Son's,
to God the Spirit of their love
be homage evermore.

To God with Gladness Sing
Psalm 95 (94)
66 66 88

To God with gladness sing,
your rock and Savior bless;
within his temple bring
your songs of thankfulness!
O God of might,
to you we sing,
enthroned as King
on heaven's height!

He cradles in his hand
the heights and depths of earth;
he made the sea and land,
he brought the world to birth!
O God most high,
we are your sheep;
on us you keep
your Shepherd's eye!

Your heav'nly Father praise,
acclaim his only Son,
your voice in homage raise
to him who makes us one!
O Dove of peace,
on us descend
that strife may end
and joy increase!

Text: Psalm 95 (94): 1-7; para. by James Quinn, SJ, ©.
Possible Tunes: DARWALL'S 148TH, CAMANO (Proulx)
Topics: Church, Holy Spirit, King (God as), Majesty,
Music, Opening of Worship, Peace (Inner), Praise,
Processional, Trinity

Text: Psalm 93 (92), para. by James Quinn, SJ, ©.
Possible Tune: STROUDWATER
Topics: Creation, King (God As), Majesty

Sing a New Song
to God on High
Psalm 96 (95)
LM

Sing a new song to God on high!
Sing the new song that is his due!
Sing of the wonders of his power!
Sing of his love, so old, so new!

Sing of the deeds his hands have wrought,
sending salvation from above,
showing to all the ends of earth
his perfect truth, his steadfast love!

Israel, sing your song of joy!
Sing while unending ages run!
Sing to the Lord with loving heart,
Israel, God's beloved son!

Sing your new song to God, our King,
praising his everlasting name!
All the wide world has seen his might:
nations of earth, tell forth his fame!

Thunder his mighty praise, O sea!
Rivers, in sunlit dance rejoice!
Echo his name, O ancient hills!
Sing, all the world, with joyful voice!

Sing to the living Lord of hosts!
Now is his flag of peace unfurled!
Justice he brings to all on earth,
God, who is King of all the world!

Sing, All Creation
Psalm 100 (99)
11 11 11 5

Sing, all creation, sing to God in gladness!
Joyously serve him, singing hymns of homage!
Chanting his praises, come before his presence!
Praise the Almighty!

Know that our God is Lord of all the ages!
He is our maker; we are all his creatures,
people he fashioned, sheep he leads to pasture!
Praise the Almighty!

Enter his temple, ringing out his praises!
Sing in thanksgiving as you come before him!
Blessing his bounty, glorify his greatness!
Praise the Almighty!

Great in his goodness is the Lord we worship;
steadfast his kindness, love that knows no ending!
Faithful his word is, changeless, everlasting!
Praise the Almighty!

Text: Psalm 96 (95), para. by James Quinn, SJ, ©.
Possible Tune: DANIEL
Topics: Majesty of God, Music, Praise, Thanksgiving

Text: Psalm 100 (99), para. by James Quinn, SJ, ©.
Possible Tune: ISTE CONFESSOR (ROUEN)
Topics: Creation, Music, Opening of Worship, Praise,
Processional

How Full of Kindness
Is the Lord
Psalm 116 (114-115)
CM

How full of kindness is the Lord,
how gracious is my God!
How good to humble hearts is he,
who saved me in my need!

My soul, be peaceful, take your rest,
so loving is the Lord;
his outstretched hand led me from death,
and wiped away my tears.

How can I thank the Lord, my God,
for all his bounteous deeds?
The cup of blessing I will take,
and praise his glorious name.

Praise the Lord,
All You Nations
Psalm 117 (116)
77 77

Praise the Lord, all you nations,
praise the Lord, all you peoples:
we have witnessed his mercy,
he is faithful for ever.

Praise the Father, who made us,
praise the Son, who redeemed us,
praise their life-giving Spirit,
praise one God through all ages.

> *Response*
> May the angels go with you
> to the home of God's glory;
> may the saints bid you welcome
> to the land of the living.
> *or*
> I shall go to God's temple,
> where the angels adore him;
> I shall go to his dwelling ,
> and rejoice in his presence.

Text: Psalm 116 (114-115); para. by James Quinn, SJ, ©.
Possible Tune: STRACATHRO
Topics: Funerals, Offertory, Praise, Redemption,
     Salvation

Text: Psalm 117 (116), para. by James Quinn, SJ, ©.
Scripture Reference: Psalm 116
Topics: Benediction, Funerals

Come, Praise the Lord
Psalm 117 (116)
14 14 478

Come, praise the Lord, the Almighty, the King of
    all nations!
Tell forth his fame, O you peoples, with loud
    acclamations!
His love is sure;
faithful his word shall endure,
steadfast through all generations!

Praise to the Father most gracious, the Lord of
    creation!
Praise to his Son, the Redeemer who wrought our
    salvation!
O heav'nly Dove,
praise to you, fruit of their love,
Giver of all consolation!

Give Thanks to the Lord
for His Goodness
Psalm 118 (117)
96 96 with refrain

Response
Rejoice, all the world, at the rising
of your King from the dead.

Give thanks to the Lord for his goodness,
for his love knows no end;
sing, Israel, songs to his greatness,
for his love knows no end.

Sing, priests of the Lord, to his glory,
for his love knows no end;
sing, all who revere the Almighty,
for his love knows no end.

The Lord with his right hand has triumphed:
he had raised me to life;
the Lord with his right hand had triumphed:
I will live his praise.

The stone that was spurned for the building
is its keystone of strength;
this work is the work of God's glory,
and a marvel to all.

This day is the day of his making,
day of gladness and joy;
give thanks to the Lord for his goodness,
for his love knows no end.

Text: Psalm 117 (116), para. by James Quinn, SJ, ©.
Possible Tune: LOBE DEN HERREN
Topics: Benediction, Faithfulness of God, Opening of
    Worship, Praise, Processional

Text: Psalm 118 (117), para. by James Quinn, SJ, ©.
Topics: Love (God's to us), Music, Praise and
    Adoration, Thanksgiving

My Heart Was on Fire
Psalm 122 (121)
96 96 with refrain

Response
Jerusalem, fairest of cities,
you are mother of all.

My heart was on fire when they told me:
"We will go to God's house!"
and now we are standing as pilgrims
in the city of peace!

Jerusalem, walled as a city,
you are circled with strength;
you gather your children in safety
in the arms of your love.

Jerusalem, welcome your pilgrims
from the tribes of the Lord,
obeying the law of God's people,
giving thanks in his house.

In Zion, the city of David,
stood the throne of the Lord,
and judgement went forth out of Zion
from the house of the King.

O pray for the peace of God's city:
"On your friends be his peace!"
"May peace be the queen in your ramparts,
may she reign in your midst!"

For love of my friends and my brethren
I will pray for your peace;
for love of God's Temple on Zion
I will pray for your good.

To You I Lift My Eyes, Dear Lord
Psalm 123 (122)
CM

To you I lift my eyes, dear Lord,
my King in heav'n above;
to you I look as children look
for help from father's hands.

As eyes of children look in need
to mother's loving hands,
so do we look to God, our Lord,
to be our friend in need.

Stretch forth your hand in love, O Lord,
on us, your little flock;
so shall we sing your loving care
now and for evermore.

Text: Psalm 123 (122), para. by James Quinn, SJ, ©.
Possible Tune: JACKSON
Topics: Children, Guidance, Shepherd, Trust

Text: Psalm 122 (121), para. by James Quinn, SJ, ©.
Topics: Biblical Names (Jerusalem), Peace (Inner)

All Your Building Is Vain
Psalm 127 (126)
67 67

Response
Those who weep as they sow
will rejoice at the harvest:
give your thanks to the Lord,
who brings joy out of sorrow.

All your building is vain
unless God is the builder;
all your watching is vain
unless God is the watchman.

You may rise before the dawn,
seek your bed after nightfall,
and yet labour in vain,
for the Lord gives the increases.

In his love God makes rich
by his present of children,
who, like arrows in flight,
will be swift to protect you.

What a blessing God gives
in this quiver of arrows
when the enemy stands
in the gate of the city.

From Depths of Grief I Cry
Psalm 130 (129)
SM

From depths of grief I cry;
on you, O Lord, I call:
give pity's ear to sorrow's plea!
O comfort my distress!

If you record our sins,
who, Lord, shall guiltless stand?
In holy fear we serve you, Lord
from whom all pardon flows.

Your word is my sure hope;
more eagerly I wait
than watchman on the city wall
awaits the light of dawn.

Let Israel keep watch
for you, O Lord, her hope,
and look more eagerly for you
than watchman looks for dawn.

With you is perfect love;
from you all peace descends;
from all her sins shall Israel
be freed by you, her Lord.

To Father, and to Son,
to Spirit, Dove of peace,
to God, who lives and loves and saves,
for evermore be praise!

Text: Psalm 130 (129), para. James Quinn, SJ, ©.
Possible Tune: ST. BRIDE
Topics: Funerals, Holy Souls

Text: Psalm 127 (126), para. by James Quinn, SJ, ©.
Topics: Providence, Thanksgiving

Lord, in My Heart
Are Simple Thoughts
Psalm 131 (130)
CM

Lord, in my heart are simple thoughts;
no room is there for pride;
with downcast eyes I humbly lay
all high concerns aside.

Now is my spirit weaned from care,
like child on mother's breast;
my soul at last is now content,
as in my God I rest.

Israel, trust your God and Lord,
both now and all your days;
place all your hope in him who saves;
let him be all your praise.

Peace is his gift who calms our fear,
who hears before we call
on Father, Son, and gentle Dove,
one gracious Lord of all.

I Call, O Lord, on You
Psalm 141 (140)
SM

I call, O Lord, on you:
come quickly to my aid,
hear from your throne in heav'n above
my cry of deep distress.

Lord, let my prayer ascend
like incense in your sight;
see in my hands to heav'n above
my evening sacrifice.

Set, Lord, a guard to keep
close watch upon my mouth;
let no rebellious word escape
your seal upon my lips.

Have pity, Lord, on me;
you are my strength, my shield:
you are my refuge in all ills;
I turn in trust to you.

I bless the Father's name;
I bless the Savior-Son;
I bless the Spirit of their love,
my solace in distress.

Text: James Quinn, SJ, based on Psalm 131 (130).
Possible Tune: ELGIN
Topics: Comfort, Evening, Humility, Trust in God

Text: Psalm 141 (140); para. by James Quinn, SJ, ©.
Possible Tune: SOUTHWELL
Topics: Comfort, Evening, Guidance

The Lord I Will Praise
Psalm 146 (145)
55 55 65 65

The Lord I will praise
as long as I live.
To him I will sing
till life is no more.
The Lord is the maker
of heaven and earth,
of rivers and ocean
and all that they hold.

The Lord God of heav'n
is steadfast in faith.
To all who are wronged
he shows himself just.
The poor and the hungry
he feeds with his bread.
He frees from their prisons
the captives in chains.

He opens the eyes
of those who are blind.
He lifts up the heads
that bow in their grief.
He shelters the stranger,
the friendless befriends.
For widow and orphan
he cares in his love.

The Lord loves the just
who work out his will.
The wicked he foils;
they stumble and fall.
For ever and ever
the Lord will be King,
Enthroned upon Zion,
till time is no more.

Praise God, O Heav'n, in Heaven's Height
Psalm 148
LM

Praise God, O heav'n, in heaven's height;
praise him, O hosts of angels bright!
Give praise, O stars, give praise, O moon,
give praise, O sun at highest noon!

Give praise to him by whose decree,
O sky above, you came to be!
O earth and sea and everything
that lives in you, his praises sing!

Praise him, O fire, praise him, O hail;
praise him, O snow and frost and gale!
Give praise, O hills that soar in air;
give praise, O woods and orchards fair!

All living things, both wild and tame,
on earth, in air, praise his great name!
O young in years, O full of days,
with one voice sing his endless praise!

O nations, praise your glorious king!
Both great and small, your homage bring;
let all the world with one accord
acclaim with joy its gracious Lord!

Text: Psalm 146 (145):2, 6-10;
    para. by James Quinn, SJ, ©.
Possible Tune: OLD 104TH
Topics: Faithfulness of God, Justice, Opening of
    Worship, Praise, Processional, Trust in God

Text: Psalm 148; para. by James Quinn, SJ, ©.
Possible Tune: SOLOTHURN
Topics: Creation, Praise

The Lord Is the God Who Saves Me
Isaiah 12:1-6
CM with refrain

Response
O sing of the Lord who saves us
in the love of his heart.

The Lord is the God who saves me,
whom I trust without fear.
The Lord is my strength, my Savior,
and the song on my lips.

With joy you will draw salvation
from the fountain of God.
Give thanks to the Lord almighty,
sing your praise of his name.

Make known in the world his wonders,
to the ends of the earth.
Proclaim to the world his greatness,
sing a psalm to his name.

Sing, Zion, your song of gladness,
and rejoice in the Lord.
The Lord, who alone is holy,
reigns in Zion, your God.

Now Is the Hour of Rejoicing
Isaiah 35:1-2, 5-10
87 87

Now is the hour of rejoicing:
desert and wasteland, be glad,
blossom with flowers as a garden;
wilderness, sing in your joy.

Lebanon, Sharon, and Carmel
lend you their beauty and grace:
bathed in the glory around you,
gaze on the splendor of God.

Eyes that are blind shall be opened;
ears that are deaf be unsealed;
feet of the lame shall be dancing;
lips that are dumb shall sing praise.

Rivers shall run in the desert,
streams in the dry land shall flow,
lakes shall appear in the wasteland,
springs in the waterless sand.

Now is prepared a King's highway
(holy is he who shall come),
ready the way for the ransomed,
road for the exiles' return.

Joyful their journey to Zion,
homecoming bless'd with delight,
gladness shall be their companion,
sorrow and tears are no more.

Mother of Carmel, in glory
sing to the Father of light,
sing to your Son, the Anointed,
sing to the Gift of their love.

Text: Isaiah 35:1-2, 5-10; para. by James Quinn, SJ, ©.
Possible Tune: CARMEL I AND II
Topics: Advent, Biblical Names (Carmel, Sharon,
Lebanon), Creation, Morning, New Heaven

Text: Isaiah 12:1-6, para. by James Quinn, SJ, ©.
Topics: Music, Praise and Adoration, Salvation, Trust

Our Heav'nly Father, May Your Name
Matthew 6:9-13
88 86

Our heav'nly Father, may your name
in every heart be bless'd and praised;
to sing your goodness, holy God,
let every voice be raised.

In glory may your Kingdom come,
when perfect love to you is giv'n;
may all on earth obey your will
as angels in high heav'n.

Give us today the food we need,
the Bread of life from heav'n above;
you are the Father of the poor,
show us a Father's love.

Forgive our sins as we forgive
all those who do us any wrong;
be with us when our flesh is weak,
by grace make weakness strong.

From every evil keep us safe,
from every danger, every fear;
drive far away the Evil One.
hear us, our Father dear.

Text: *The Lord's Prayer* (Matthew 6:9-13),
    para. by James Quinn, SJ, ©.
Possible Tune: CHILDHOOD
Topics: Forgiveness, Prayer

O Praise, My Soul, the Lord
Luke 1:46-55 *Magnificat*
SM

O praise, my soul, the Lord!
O glorify his name!
In him my spirit thrills with joy,
my Savior and my God!

From heav'n he gazed on me,
his lowly servant-maid;
behold, all ages yet to come
shall call me blest of God!

The Lord of wondrous power
has done great things for me;
for ever blessed be his name
who is the holy One!

His mercy he reveals,
to those who fear his name;
from age to age his steadfast love
shall endlessly endure!

His arm is strong to save!
he scatters all the proud;
he casts the mighty from their thrones;
he raises up the meek!

He fills the hungry poor
with blessings from above;
the rich he strips of wealth and power
and empty sends away!

His mighty hand has grasped
the hand of Israel,
his servant-son, beloved by him
with never-failing love!

Now is his promise kept,
once made to Abraham,
that in his seed we would be blest
for all eternity!

O Father, fount of joy,
your glory I adore!
O loving Spirit, praise be yours,
who gave me God, my Son!

Text: *Magnificat* (*Song of Mary*–Luke 1:46-55),
    para. by James Quinn, SJ, ©.
Possible Tune: EDWIN
Topics: Mary, Praise and Adoration

Blessed Be the God of Israel
Luke 1:68-79 *Benedictus*
CM (CMD)

Blessed be the God of Israel,
the ever-living Lord.
who comes in power to save his own,
his people Israel.

For Israel you now raise up
salvation's tower on high
in David's house, who reigned as king
and servant of the Lord.

Through holy prophets did he speak
his word from days of old,
that he would save us from our foes
and all who bear us ill.

On Sinai he gave to us
his covenant of love;
so with us now he keeps his word
in love that knows no end.

Of old he swore his solemn oath
to father Abraham;
from him a mighty race should spring,
one bless'd for evermore.

He swore to set his people free
from fear of every foe
that we might serve him all our days
in goodness, love, and peace.

O tiny child, your name shall be
the prophet of the Lord;
the way for God you shall prepare
to make his coming known.

You shall proclaim to Israel
salvation's dawning day,
when God shall wipe away our sins
in his redeeming love.

The rising Sun shall shine on us
to bring the light of day
to all who sit in darkest night
and shadow of the grave.

Our footsteps God shall safely guide
to walk the ways of peace.
his name for evermore be bless'd
who lives and loves and saves.

Text: *Benedictus* (*Song of Zechariah*, Luke 1:68-79),
para. by James Quinn, SJ, 1990, ©.
Possible Tune: CHESHIRE; THIRD MODE MELODY; FOREST
GREEN (CMD)
Topics: Advent, Biblical names (Abraham, Zachariah),
Covenant, Guidance, Morning, Promises, Salvation

Lord, Bid Your Servant Go in Peace
Luke 2:29-32, 34-35
Nunc Dimittis
CM

Lord, bid your servant go in peace,
your word is now fulfilled.
These eyes have seen salvation's dawn,
this Child so long foretold.

This is the Savior of the world,
the Gentiles' promised light,
God's glory dwelling in our midst,
the joy of Israel.

This Child shall see in Israel,
so many rise or fall:
God's sign raised high for all to see,
which yet shall be denied.

His mother's soul a sword shall pierce,
of sorrow, keen and deep.
From many hearts their secret thoughts
through him shall be revealed.

Bless'd be the Father, who has giv'n
his Son to be our Lord;
bless'd too that Son, and with them both
the Spirit of their love.

You Give, Lord, the Sign to Your Servant
Luke 2:29-32 *Nunc Dimittis*
95 95 with response

Response
May God give his grace in our waking
and watch as we sleep;
may Christ be our Friend in the daylight,
our peace through the night.

You give, Lord, the sign to your servant
to go in your peace;
your promise of old has been honored,
your word has been fulfilled.

At last I have seen your salvation,
your gift to the world;
the light of the Gentiles, the glory
in Israel's midst.

Give thanks to the Father of mercies,
give thanks to his Son,
give thanks to the joy-giving Spirit,
give thanks to one God.

Text: *Nunc dimittis* (*Song of Simeon*, Luke 2:29-32, 34-35), trans. by James Quinn, SJ, 1969, 1989, ©.
Possible Tunes: LAND OF REST, MORNING SONG
Topics: Biblical names (Simeon), Close of Worship, Evening, Funeral

Text: *Nunc dimittis* (*Song of Simeon*, Luke 2:29-32, 34-35), trans. by James Quinn, SJ, ©.
Topics: Biblical names (Simeon), Close of Worship, Funeral

Peace, My Own Peace, Is the Gift I Leave with You
John 14:27; 15:1-12
11 11 11 11

Peace, my own peace, is the gift I leave with you;
peace I bequeath as my parting gift of love;
mine is the peace that the world cannot give;
this is the peace that I give, and I alone.

I am the vine that my Father tends with care;
each branch he prunes that the vine may bear
    more fruit;
severed from me, you will wither and die;
one with the vine, you will bear abundant fruit.

You I have loved as my Father loves his Son;
love as I love, for I do my Father's will;
do as I do, that my joy may be yours;
this is my will, that you love as I have loved.

This Is My Will
John 15:12-17
LM

This is my will, my one command,
that love should dwell among you all.
    This is my will, that you should love
    as I have shown that I love you.

No greater love can be than this:
to choose to die to save one's friends.
    You are my friends if you obey
    what I command that you should do.

I call you now no longer slaves;
no slave knows all his master does.
    I call you friends, for all I hear
    my Father say you hear from me.

You chose not me, but I chose you,
that you should go and bear much fruit.
    I chose you out that you in me
    should bear much fruit that will abide.

All that you ask my Father dear
for my name's sake you shall receive.
    This is my will, my one command,
    that love should dwell in each, in all.

Text: John 14: 27, 15:1-2, 4-6, 9-12; para. by James
    Quinn, SJ, ©.
Possible Tune: PEACE, PERFECT PEACE (Mayhew)
Topics: Communion, Love, Peace, Unity

Text: John 15:12-17, para. by James Quinn, SJ, ©.
Possible Tune: SUANTRAI
Topics: Church, Communion, Unity, Will of God

We Who Live in Christ Were Born in His Death
Romans 6:3-11
10 12 11 11

We who live in Christ were born in his death:
baptized in Christ's death, with Christ we lay in the
  tomb;
as God the Father's power awoke him from death,
so we were raised to walk in newness of life.

One with Christ were we in dying his death;
so one shall we be with Christ in rising again.
Our sinful selves were nailed with Christ to his
  cross
that, dead to sin, from sin our flesh might be free.

Dead with Christ, we yet shall rise with him, too,
for this is our faith, that he who rose from the dead
will never die; once dead, forever he lives,
and death has power no more to conquer its King.

Once for all in death Christ died to all sin;
the life that he lives is life lived only to God.
So you like him are dead to all that is sin,
and live to God in Christ, the Savior, our Lord.

How Deep the Riches of Our God
Romans 11:33-36
CM

How deep the riches of our God,
his wisdom how sublime;
how high his judgments soar above
all judgment of mankind!

What mind has read the mind of God,
or giv'n him counsel sure?
Who from his riches gave to God
what was not first received?

From God all things created flow;
all things through him exist;
to him for judgment all returns,
to whom all praise is due!

To God the Father, fount of grace,
through his beloved Son
in oneness with the Holy Ghost
be glory evermore!

Text: Romans 6:3-11, para. by James Quinn, SJ, ©.
Possible Tune: REALT NA MAIDNE
Topics: Baptism

Text: Romans 11:33-36, para. by James Quinn, SJ, ©.
Possible Tune: RICHMOND
Topics: Creation, Majesty of God, Praise, Trinity

Love Is Long-Suff'ring; Love Is Kind
I Corinthians 13:4-7
CM

Love is long-suff'ring; love is kind,
love envies not, nor boasts;
love knows not pride but courtesy;
love does not seek its own.

Love is not quick to take offence;
no bitter thought love thinks.
When others fail, love is not glad
but finds its joy in good.

Love is content to bear all ills;
in all does love believe;
in perfect trust love hopes for all;
through all shall love endure.

Let Your Might Be the Lord Almighty
Ephesians 6:10-17
98 98 96 97

Let your might be the Lord Almighty,
your strength be his strength alone.
Let your armor be all God's armor,
lest you yield to the devil's guile,
For you fight with no mortal foeman:
but ranged in rank on rank
Stand the princes of outer darkness,
high kings of a willful world.

Let the truth be your belt in battle,
make justice your breastplate bright.
Let your feet wear the shoes of swiftness,
as you spread the good news of peace.
Let the shield that is faith defend you
from harm by Satan's hosts.
Let your helmet be God's salvation,
your sword be the Spirit's word.

Text: I Corinthians 13:4-7,
    para. by James Quinn, SJ, ©.
Possible Tune: ABRIDGE
Topics: Communion, Love (God's), Marriage,
    Penitence

Text: Ephesians 6:10-17, para. by James Quinn, SJ, ©.
Possible Tune: CORMAC
Topics: Justice, Temptation, Victory, Warfare
    (Spiritual), Word

Let All Be One in Mind and Heart
Phillipians 2:5-11
CM

Christ Is the Likeness That Reveals
Colossians 1:15-20
CM

Let all be one in mind and heart
with Jesus Christ, our Lord,
who, though he was by nature God,
God's glory laid aside.

Christ is the likeness that reveals
God, whom no eye has seen.
in him creation came to be,
God's firstborn, Lord of all.

He laid his heavenly glory down;
God's Servant he became;
obediently he lived, to die
in shame upon the cross.

On him creation still depends,
heav'n, earth, things seen, unseen,
thrones, dominations, princedoms, powers,
all through him, for him, made.

Now God has raised him up, to bear
the name above all names;
at Jesus' name all knees shall bow,
all tongues proclaim him Lord.

He is before all else that is,
all is in him made whole.
He is the head who rules the Church,
one Body with its Lord.

All glory now the Father shares
with his exalted Son,
whom God the Holy Spirit raised
from death to heaven's throne.

He is the First, as firstborn Son
who rose the first from death,
who as creation's sovereign Lord
all primacy now owns.

In him God's fullness chose to dwell,
by him to make all one,
through death to bring in peace to him
all things of heav'n and earth.

Text: Phillipians 2:5-11, para. by James Quinn, SJ, ©.
Possible Tune: ST. STEPHEN (NEWINGTON)
Topics: Opening of Worship, Processional, Unity

Text: Colossians 1:15-20, para. by James Quinn, SJ, ©.
Possible Tune: LONDON NEW
Topics: Creation, King (Christ As), Praise

Risen to Life with Christ

Colossians 3:1-4

66 66 with refrain

Response
Wake from your sleep of death;
walk in the light of Christ!

Risen to life with Christ,
look to the things above,
where at the Father's side
Christ is enthroned on high.

Think on the things of heav'n,
not on the things of earth;
dead to this life, you live
hidden with Christ in God.

Christ is our hidden life;
when he at last is seen,
you will be seen with him,
sharing his glorious light.

You Appeared, O Christ

I Timothy 3:16

54 54 with refrain

Response
Alleluia, Alleluia
Praise the Lord and his Christ
with their Spirit.
Alleluia.

You appeared, O Christ,
in our nature.
You were proved God's Son
by the Spirit.

You were seen alive
by your angels.
You were preached by men
to all peoples.

You are known by faith
to the nations.
You are throned on high
in your glory.

Text: Colossians 3:1-4, para. by James Quinn, SJ, ©.
Scripture Reference–Response: Ephesians 5:14
Topics: Christian Life, Light, Resurrection

Text: I Timothy 3:16, para. by James Quinn, SJ, ©.
Topics: Faith, Praise and Adoration

Christ Gave His Life for You
I Peter 2:21-24
64 65

Response
God sent the sinless One
to die to sin,
and raise to life in him
his holy people.

Christ gave his life for you;
that you might live;
he opened up the way
for you to follow.

Sinless he lived and died,
he told no lie;
to those who hated him
he gave no answer.

Stretched on his cross of pain,
he kept his peace;
he put his trust in him
who judges justly.

Christ in his body bore
our sins to death,
that we might die to sin
and live to goodness.

Wounded, he healed our wounds
and made us whole;
when we had strayed like sheep
he sought and found us.

He is the shepherd-king
who guards his flock;
you now are one with him
in his safe keeping.

Glory to you, O God,
through Christ your Son,
one only God with you
and God the Spirit.

Text: I Peter 2:21-24, para. by James Quinn, SJ,
Scripture Reference–Response: II Corinthians 5:21
Topics: Epiphany/Life of Christ, Salvation, Shepherd

Hymns for the Church at Worship

This Day God Gives Me
55 54D

This day God gives me
strength of high heaven,
sun and moon shining,
flame in my hearth,
flashing of lightning,
wind in its swiftness,
deeps of the ocean,
firmness of earth.

This day God sends me
strength to sustain me,
might to uphold me,
wisdom as guide.
Your eyes are watchful;
your ears are listening;
your lips are speaking;
friend at my side.

God's way is my way;
God's shield is round me;
God's host defends me,
saving from ill.
Angels of heaven,
drive from me always
all that would harm me,
stand by me still.

Rising, I thank you,
mighty and strong One,
King of creation,
Giver of rest,
firmly confessing
Threeness of Persons,
Oneness of Godhead,
Trinity blest.

Text: Adapt. from *St. Patrick's Breastplate* (8th cent.)
by James Quinn, SJ, ©.
Possible Tunes: BUNESSAN, SANJEEV (Schulz-Widmar)
Topics: Christian Life, Guidance, Morning, Opening of
Worship, Processional

I Believe in God, the Father
87 87

I believe in God, the Father;
I believe in God, his Son;
I believe in God, their Spirit;
each is God, yet God is one.

I believe what God has spoken
through his Church, whose word is true;
boldly she proclaims his Gospel,
ever old, yet ever new.

All my hope is in God's goodness,
shown for us by him who died,
Jesus Christ, the world's Redeemer,
spotless Victim crucified.

All my love is Love eternal;
in that Love I love mankind.
Take my heart, O heart once broken,
take my soul, my strength, my mind.

Bless'd be God, the loving Father;
Bless'd be God, his only Son;
Bless'd be God, all-holy Spirit;
Bless'd be God, for ever one.

Father of Mercies, Heav'n's Eternal Dayspring
11 11 11 5

Father of mercies, heav'n's eternal Dayspring,
Maker of all things, shine on your creation,
visit your children, born to share your glory,
heirs of your Kingdom.

Son of the Father, splendor born of splendor,
star of the morning, sun that knows no setting,
come now in blessing, God's true Word and
　　Wisdom,
Dawn of salvation.

Spirit of Jesus, fire of love descending,
warmth of our spirit, light when all is darkness,
strength in our weakness, joy in every sorrow,
be with us always.

Text: James Quinn, SJ, ©.
Possible Tune: SUSSEX
Topics: Church, Faith, Opening of Worship,
　　Processional, Salvation, Trinity

Text: James Quinn, SJ, ©.
Possible Tunes: CHRISTE SANCTORUM, HERZLIEBSTER JESU
Topics: Morning, Trinity

Dear Father, Take from Loving Hands
CM

Dear Father, take from loving hands
our gifts of bread and wine;
from all your gifts you chose them out
to be love's perfect sign.

These gifts will be a greater gift,
the greatest we can give:
the Lamb who takes away our sins,
who died that we might live.

These are the gifts which Jesus blessed
the night before he died,
to show that he is our high priest,
for our sake crucified.

Send us the Spirit of your love
to make Christ present here,
that he may be our sacrifice,
the gift you hold most dear.

This bread will be his living self,
this wine his blood will be;
our gifts will be the perfect gift
he gave on Calvary.

This gift of gifts you will restore
to greatest and to least,
to make us one in love and joy
in your communion-feast.

O Father, Take in Sign of Love
CM

O Father, take in sign of love
these gifts of bread and wine!
With them we give our very selves
to be for ever thine!

These gifts another gift will be,
thy son in very deed,
for us a willing victim made,
the Lamb on whom we feed!

These are the gifts thy Son did bless
the night before he died,
by which he showed himself a priest
and victim crucified!

He now has given us as our own
his offering made to thee:
his Body broken, Blood outpoured,
for us on Calvary!

This bread his Body will become,
this wine his Blood will be!
Our humble gifts will be the gift
that is most dear to thee!

This perfect gift thou wilt restore
to greatest and to least,
to make all one in love and joy
in thy communion-feast!

Text: James Quinn, SJ, ©.
Possible Tune: HORSLEY
Topics: Communion, Lamb of God, Offering, Real
   Presence

Text: James Quinn, SJ, ©.
Possible Tune: HORSLEY
Topics: Communion, Lamb of God, Offertory

Loving Father, from Your Bounty
87 87 87

Loving Father, from your bounty
choicest gifts unnumbered flow;
all the blessings of salvation,
which to Christ your Son we owe,
all the gifts that by your bidding
nature's hands on us bestow.

Here your grateful children gather,
off'ring gifts of bread and wine;
these we give to you in homage,
of your love the loving sign,
and restore to you creation,
through this fruit of earth and wine.

Soon will come Christ's loving presence
on our love to set his scale,
Sacred Body, precious Life-blood,
nread and wine will then reveal;
nread and wine, though these no longer,
flesh and blood will yet conceal.

Come Down, O Spirit Blest!
66 11D

Come down, O Spirit blest!
Here on this altar rest!
Bless these our gifts and with them all creation!
Changing this bread and wine;
make them the gift divine
of Christ, our sacrifice of adoration!

Spirit of heavenly light,
shine on our inward sight,
your splendor all our darkness dispossessing!
Our hearts create anew
to offer homage due
through God's own Son, to God your love
    confessing!

Spirit of holiness,
your seal on us impress,
God's dwelling-place for ever here preparing!
make present at this feast
our everlasting priest,
his priesthood with his holy people sharing!

Text: James Quinn, SJ, ©.
Possible Tune: PICARDY
Topics: Gifts (God's), Offering, Communion

Text: James Quinn, SJ, ©.
Possible Tunes: SIGHTHILL, ST. BRUNO
Topics: Communion, Offertory

To God Our Father, Sovereign Lord

88 88 88

To God our Father, sovereign Lord,
with joy let all creation sing;
the homage of creation's gifts
with grateful hearts his creatures bring;
to him we offer bread and wine
through Christ, creation's Priest and King.

Of many grains this bread is made
from harvest-fields of golden corn;
ground by the millstone, each has died
to be as purest bread reborn,
bread that will die to rise as Christ,
who rose from death on Easter morn.

Grapes in the winepress died to fill
this holy chalice with its wine,
wine that will die to rise once more
as Blood of Christ, salvation's sign,
blood that will flow through branch and grape
as life-blood of the mystic vine.

With Christ, our head, we all have died,
baptized in Blood for sinners shed,
to rise with him who rose again
as glorious Firstborn from the dead;
the many now are one in Christ,
one Body nourished by one Bread.

Come, Holy Spirit, make our hearts
with Christ's own heart for ever one!
Upon these gifts descend in power,
make them the Father's firstborn Son,
that as one Body we may share
one Bread of Life till life be done.

King of Angels, You Are Welcome

87 87

King of angels, you are welcome,
risen Body that feeds my own.
Take my body, take my spirit,
make them yours and yours alone.

Body born of Virgin Mother,
Child of promise, yet God the Son,
welcome, heart's desire, true Wisdom,
make us holy, make us one.

Text: James Quinn, SJ, ©.
Possible Tune: WER NUR DEN LIEBEN GOTT
Scripture Reference: I Corinthians 10:16-17
Topics: Communion, Offertory

Text: *Fáilte romhat;* trans. by James Quinn, SJ, 1991, ©.
Possible Tune: FÁILTE ROMHAT
Topics: Communion, Offertory

Bless'd Be the Lord Our God
SMD

Bless'd be the Lord our God!
With joy let heaven ring;
before his presence let all earth
its songs of homage bring!
His mighty deeds be told;
his majesty be praised;
to God, enthroned in heav'nly light,
let every voice be raised!

All that has life and breath,
give thanks with heartfelt songs!
To him let all creation sing
to whom all praise belongs!
Acclaim the Father's love,
who gave us God his Son;
Praise too the Spirit, giv'n by both,
with both for ever one!

I Am the Holy Vine
66 66 44 44

I am the holy vine,
which God my Father tends.
each branch that yields no fruit
my Father cuts away.
Each fruitful branch
he prunes with care
to make it yield
abundant fruit.

If you abide in me,
I will in you abide.
Each branch to yield its fruit
must with the vine be one.
so you shall fail
to yield your fruit
if you are not
with me one vine.

I am the fruitful vine,
and you my branches are.
If you abide in me,
I will in you abide.
so shall you yield
much fruit, but none
if you remain
apart from me.

Text: James Quinn, SJ, based on Psalm 150.
Possible Tune: DIADEMATA
Topics: Communion, Praise, Thanksgiving, Trinity

Text: John 15:1-2, 4-5; para. by James Quinn, SJ, ©.
Possible Tunes: LITTLE CONRAD, LOVE UNKNOWN
Topics: Christian Life, Communion

I Am the Bread of Life
66 66D

I am the Bread of Life,
not as that bread of old:
your fathers manna ate,
they ate, and they are dead.
This is the Bread from heav'n;
who eats it shall not die;
I am the living Bread,
the true Bread from above.

The Bread that I will give
shall be my living flesh,
my flesh, which I will give
in death for all the world.
In truth I say to you:
unless you eat my flesh,
unless you drink my blood,
you have not life in you.

Whoever eats my flesh,
whoever drinks my blood,
has everlasting life,
and I will raise him up.
My flesh is food indeed;
my blood is drink indeed;
who eats and drinks of me
dwells in me, I in him.

His Son, who lives by him,
the living Father sent;
so all who eat of me
shall live by my own life.
From heaven bread came down;
your fathers ate, and died.
This Bread that I will give
eat, and for ever live.

The Bread That We Break
12 11 12 11

The Bread that we break makes us one in Christ's
    Body;
the Cup that we bless makes us one in his Blood;
this Bread and this Wine are the food of one Body.
Christ makes all one through his Flesh and his
    Blood.

Once many, we now are one Bread of Christ's
    Body;
like wheat that is ground we are made but one
    Bread.
Once many, we form but one Wine in this chalice,
like grapes we are one in the Wine of his Blood.

Text: I Corinthians 10:16-17, para. by James Quinn, SJ, ©.
Possible Tune: WAS LEBET, WAS SCHWEBET
Topics: Blood of Christ, Body of Christ, Communion

Bless'd Are You, O Poor in Spirit
LMD

Bless'd are you, O poor in spirit:
here is wealth beyond all telling!
Bless'd are you that faint with hunger:
here is Food, all want dispelling!
Bless'd are you that weep for sorrow:
endless gladness here is given!
Bless'd are you when all shall hate you:
I will be your joy in heaven!

Text: John 6:48-51, 53-58; para. by James Quinn, SJ, ©.
Possible Tune: O MENTES PERFIDAS
Topics: Blood of Christ, Body of Christ, Communion,
    Funerals

Text: Luke 6:20-23; para. by James Quinn, SJ, ©.
Possible Tune: SCHMÜCKE DICH
Topics: Communion, Gifts of God

Forth from on High the Father Sends
LM

Forth from on high the Father sends
his Son, who yet stays by his side.
The Word made us for us then spends
his life till life's last eventide.

While Judas plans the traitor's sign,
the mocking kiss that Love betrays,
Jesus in form of bread and wine
his loving sacrifice displays.

He gives himself that faith may see
the heavenly Food on which we feed,
that flesh and blood in us may be
fed by his Flesh and Blood in deed.

By birth he makes himself man's kin;
as Food before his guests he lies;
to death he bears the cross of sin;
in heaven he reigns as our best prize.

O Priest and Victim, Lord of Life,
throw wide the gates of Paradise!
We face our foes in mortal strife;
you are our strength! O heed our cries!

To Father, Son and Spirit blest,
one only God, be ceaseless praise!
May he in goodness grant us rest
in heaven, our home, for endless days!
Amen.

Text: *Verbum Supernum*, St. Thomas Aquinas;
  trans. by James Quinn, SJ, ©.
Possible Tune: MELCOMBE
Topics: Benediction, Biblical Names (Judas),
  Communion

Hail Our Savior's Glorious Body
87 87 87

Hail our Savior's glorious Body,
which his Virgin Mother bore;
hail the Blood which, shed for sinners,
did a broken world restore;
hail the sacrament most holy,
flesh and Blood of Christ adore!

To the Virgin for our healing,
his own Son the Father sends;
from the Father's love proceeding
sower, seed, and Word descends;
wondrous life of Word incarnate
with his greatest wonder ends!

On that paschal evening see him
with the chosen twelve recline,
to the old law still obedient
in its feast of love divine;
love divine, the new law giving,
gives himself as Bread and Wine!

By his word the Word almighty
makes of bread his flesh indeed;
wine becomes his very life-blood;
faith God's living Word must heed!
Faith alone may safely guide us
where the senses cannot lead!

Come, adore this wondrous presence;
bow to Christ, the source of grace!
Here is kept the ancient promise
of God's earthly dwelling-place!
Sight is blind before God's glory,
faith alone may see his face!

Glory be to God the Father,
praise to his coequal Son,
adoration to the Spirit,
bond of love, in Godhead one!
Blest be God by all creation
joyously while ages run!

Text: *Pange, lingua, gloriosi Corporis,* St. Thomas
  Aquinas; trans. by James Quinn, SJ, ©.
Possible Tunes: PRAISE, MY SOUL; Mode III Plainsong
Topics: Benediction, Communion, Presence (God's),
  Word of God

Jesus, Redeemer, from Your Heart
LM

Jesus, Redeemer, from your Heart,
wounded by love, all graces flow.
Your greatest gift to us impart:
your living self on us bestow.

This crowning gift escapes our sight:
faith bids us lovingly recall
how on that wondrous paschal night,
loving your own, you gave your all.

King who is throned above the skies,
ruling the world with royal sway,
lowly you knelt in servant's guise,
washing the stains of guilt away.

Bread you did bless: "Take this and eat:
this is my Body, which is given
for all of you." O words most sweet!
Hail, blessed Body, Bread from heaven!

Wine you did bless to give us cheer:
"This is the Chalice of my Blood,
shed for you all." O words most dear!
O broken Heart! O cleansing flood!

Praise be to you, our Host and Guest,
Jesus, our Blessed Lady's Son,
to Father and to Spirit blest,
Praise to one God while ages run.

At This Great Feast of Love
66 84D

At this great feast of love
let joyful praise resound,
let heartfelt homage now ascend
to heaven's height:
ring out the reign of sin;
ring in the reign of grace;
a world renewed acclaims its King,
though veiled from sight.

Recall that night when Christ
proclaims his law of love,
and shows himself as Lamb of God
and great high priest:
the sinless One, made sin,
for sinners gives his all,
and shares with us his very self
as Paschal feast.

The bread that angels eat
becomes our food on earth,
God sends his manna, living Bread,
from heav'n above;
what wonders now we see:
those who are last and least
receive their Lord as food and drink,
his pledge of love.

Three persons, yet one God,
be pleased to hear our prayer:
come down in pow'r to seek your own,
dispel our night;
teach us your word of truth;
guide us along your way;
bring us at last to dwell with you
in endless light.

Text: James Quinn, SJ, ©.
Possible Tune: TUGWOOD
Scripture References: st. 3, John 13:1-20, 34-35
Topics: Communion, Salvation

Text: *Sacris sollemniis*, St. Thomas Aquinas;
trans. by James Quinn, SJ, 1988, ©.
Possible Tune: LEONI
Topics: Body of Christ, Communion

Now on This Feast of Love
12 12 12 8

Now on this feast of love let there be joyful praise,
homage from thankful hearts rising to heaven's
     throne.
Ring out the reign of sin; ring in the reign of
     Christ,
world renewed by his gift of grace.

Here we recall the night when with his chosen
     friends
Christ kept the Paschal feast, giving his law of love,
night when the Lamb of God offered in sacrifice
Body broken and Blood outpoured.

Bread on which angels feast, now is our food on
     earth,
promised from days of old, true Bread from heav'n
     above.
Marvel of marvels to see: those who are last and
     least
feed on him who is Lord of all.

One God in Trinity, graciously hear our prayer:
come with you healing pow'r, make us your
     dwelling-place,
teach us your word of truth; guide us along your
     way,
lead us home to your endless light.

Christ the King, Enthroned in Splendor
87 87 77

Christ the King, enthroned in splendor,
comes from heaven to be our priest!
One with him as priest and victim,
one in love, we share his feast!
Praise him in high heaven above!
Praise him in this feast of love!

Light here scatters all our darkness!
Life here triumphs over death!
Come, receive from Christ in glory
God the Spirit's living breath!
Praise Christ for his victory won!
Praise the Father's firstborn Son!

Heaven is here! The gracious Father
gives to us his only Son!
Here is sent the loving Spirit,
making all in Christ but one!
Praise the Father, praise the Son,
praise the Spirit, Godhead one!

Text: *Sacris sollemniis*, St. Thomas Aquinas;
     trans. by James Quinn, SJ, ©.
Topics: Benediction, Communion, Maundy Thursday

Text: James Quinn, SJ, ©.
Possible Tunes: ALL SAINTS, LATIMER (Landis)
Topics: Ascension and Reign, Communion,
     King (Christ As), Light, Trinity

Here in Christ We Gather
12 12 12 12 with refrain

Where True Love Is Dwelling
11 11

God is love, and where true love is
God himself is there.

Where true love is dwelling, God is dwelling there;
love's own loving Presence love does ever share.

Here in Christ we gather, love of Christ our calling.
Christ, our love, is with us, gladness be his
greeting.
Let us love and serve him, God of all the ages.
Let us love sincerely, seeing Christ in others.

Love of Christ has made us out of many one;
in our midst is dwelling God's eternal Son.

God is love, and where true love is
God himself is there.

Give Him joyful welcome, love Him and revere;
Cherish one another with a love sincere.

When we Christians gather, members of one Body,
Christ, our Head, is with us, loving and beloved.
Here is sent the Spirit, one with Son and Father,
fire of love's indwelling, bond of peace among us.

As in Christ we gather discord has no part;
ours is but one spirit, but one mind and heart.

God is love, and where true love is
God himself is there.

Bitterness now ended, let there be accord;
always with us dwelling be our God and Lord.

Grant us love's fulfillment, joy with all the blessed,
when we see your glory, risen Lord and Savior.
Bathe us in your splendor, Light of all creation,
be our bliss forever as we sing your praises.

May we share the vision with the saints on high
of Christ's matchless glory when we come to die.

Joy of all the blessed, be our heav'nly prize;
dwell with us for ever, Lord of Paradise!

God is love, and where true love is
God himself is there.

Where true love is dwelling, God is dwelling there;
love's own loving Presence love does ever share.

Text: *Ubi Caritas et Amor,* from the Liturgy of
    Maundy Thursday; tr. by James Quinn, SJ, 1988, ©.
Possible Tunes: UBI CARITAS, MANDATUM
Scripture References: John 13:1-20, 34-35
Topics: Communion, Maundy Thursday, Offertory

Text: *Ubi caritas;* trans. by James Quinn, SJ, ©.
Possible Tune: GLENFINLAS
Scripture References: John 13:1-20, 34-35
Topics: Church, Communion, Unity

Jesus, in Death You Shed Your Blood
CM

Jesus, in death you shed your Blood
that each of us might live;
now as our living Bread from heav'n
your loving self you give.

Jesus, we see you present here
by faith and not by sight;
love bids you welcome, living Bread,
in whom is all delight.

Jesus, you give your very all,
true Bread from heav'n above;
you are the giver and the gift,
yhe sign, the source, of love.

How can we thank you, loving Lord,
who show yourself so kind?
Take what we have, take all we are,
our heart, our strength, our mind.

These are the gifts we now restore
to you, our Lord and King;
since you have shared your all with us
to you our all we bring.

Jesus, Lord of Glory
11 11 11 11

Jesus, Lord of glory, clothed in heaven's light,
here I bow before you, hidden from my sight.
King to whom my body, mind, and heart belong,
mind and heart here falter, Love so deep, so strong.

Here distrust, my spirit, eye and tongue and hand,
trust faith's ear and listen, hear and understand.
Hear the voice of Wisdom, speaking now to you;
when God's Word has spoken, what can be more
    true?

Once you hid your glory, Jesus crucified;
now you hide your body, Jesus glorified.
When you come in judgment, plain for all to see,
God and man in splendor; Lord, remember me.

Once you showed to Thomas wounded hands and
    side;
here I kneel adoring, faith alone my guide.
Help me grow in faith, Lord, grow in hope and love,
living by your Spirit, gift of God above.

Here I see your dying, Jesus, victim-priest;
here I know your rising, host and guest and feast.
Let me taste your goodness, manna from the skies;
feed me, heal me, save me, food of Paradise.

Heart of Jesus, broken, pierced, and opened wide,
wash me in the water flowing from your side.
Jesus' blood, so precious that one drop could free
all the world from evil, come and ransom me.

How I long to see you, Jesus, face to face,
how my heart is thirsting, living spring of grace.
Show me soon your glory, be my great reward,
be my joy for ever, Jesus, gracious Lord.

Text: *Adoro te devote*, St. Thomas Aquinas;
    trans. by James Quinn, SJ, ©.
Possible Tune: ADORO TE DEVOTE (Plainsong)
Topics: Benediction, Communion, Real Presence

N.B. The meter has been regularized by omitting the
    extra first syllable in the Latin.

Text: James Quinn, SJ, ©.
Possible Tune: NUN DANKET ALL
Topics: Blood of Christ, Communion, Offertory
    (ommitting st. 2), Presence (God's)

King, from Your Royal Throne
66 66 with refrain

Response
Deep in our hearts, O King,
be King in your Kingdom.

King, from your royal throne
your visit your people.
Here in this royal gift
you come in your Kingship.

Lord, you invite your guests
to share in your banquet.
You are our Bread of life,
the Wine of our gladness.

You are the King of kings,
yet share with us kingship.
Here in this kingly meal
you serve us, your servants.

Give us in heaven's joy
the glory of kingship.
Gather from East to West
the heirs of your Kingdom.

Come, Christ's Beloved
10 10

Come, Christ's beloved, feed on Christ's true flesh;
drink your redemption in his precious blood.

Here is salvation, here the risen Lord,
here God's great banquet: let us thank our God.

Christ in this myst'ry gives his flesh and blood,
guiding us safely through death's gates to life.

Son of the Father, Lord of all the world,
Christ is our Savior through his cross and blood.

Christ, priest and victim, gave himself for all,
at once the giver and his gift divine.

Priests of the old law, off'ring blood outpour'd,
did but foreshadow Christ, the victim-priest.

Christ, our salvation, Christ, the light of all,
has yet enriched us by this gift sublime.

Bring to this banquet faithful hearts sincere;
receive the safeguard of eternal life.

Christ, ever-watchful shepherd of his sheep,
gives true believers life that knows no end.

Christ gives the hungry heav'nly bread to eat;
he gives the thirsty living springs of grace.

Alpha, the firstborn, Omega the end,
you came as Savior, you will come as Judge.

Come, Christ's beloved, feed on Christ's true flesh;
drink your redemption in his precious blood.

Text: From the *Antiphonary of Bennchar* (7th cent.);
trans. by James Quinn, SJ, ©.
Possible Tune: SONG 22
Topics: Communion, Real Presence, Presence (God's)

Text: James Quinn, SJ, ©.
Topics: Communion, King (God as)

Jesus' Soul, Make Holy
66 66

Jesus' soul, make holy
souls by sin made lowly;
Jesus' body, feed us
and to heaven lead us.

Lifeblood for us flowing,
set our hearts aglowing;
cleanse us, water streaming
for the world's redeeming.

Bitter passion, cheer us;
O good Jesus, hear us;
in your wounds receive us;
Jesus, never leave us.

From our foe defend us;
in death's hour befriend us;
bid us then possess you,
evermore to bless you.

O Food to Pilgrims Given
76 76D

O food to pilgrims given,
O bread that angels eat,
O manna, joy of heaven,
to every taste so sweet,
O Love all love inspiring,
thy sweetness never cloys,
thou art our whole desiring,
the pledge of heaven's joys!

O purest stream outflowing
from Love's sore-wounded heart,
O lifeblood richly glowing,
Our life, our hope, thou art!
O how our hearts are burning,
with thirst for thee on fire!
Our love, O Love, returning,
fulfill our one desire!

O Jesus, humbly hidden
from mortal eye and ear,
as thou thyself hast bidden
we own thy presence here!
This heav'nly Bread conceals thee;
by faith alone we see
till heaven's light reveals thee
in all thy majesty!

Text: *Anima Christi*, 14th cent.; trans. by James
    Quinn, SJ, ©.
Possible Tune: RAVENSHAW
Topics: Benediction, Communion, Real Presence

Text: *O esca viatorum*, 17th cent.; trans. by James
    Quinn, SJ, ©.
Possible Tune: AURELIA
Topics: Benediction, Communion, Real Presence

O Food for Pilgrims Lowly
776 776

O food for pilgrims lowly,
O angels' bread all-holy,
O manna of the blest!
with heavenly sweetness filling
our hearts, to thy love thrilling,
stay with us, loving guest!

O fount of love past knowing,
O purest stream outflowing
from Jesus' sacred heart!
Our thirsting souls inviting,
alone our hearts delighting,
our joy of joys thou art!

O Jesus we adore thee
as here we kneel before thee,
though hidden from our sight!
The veils of sense conceal thee;
may death at last reveal thee
in heaven's eternal light!

Text: *O esca viatorum*, 17th cent.;
    trans. by James Quinn, SJ, ©.
Possible Tunes: IN ALLEN MEINEN, THATEN
Topics: Benediction, Communion, Real Presence

O Sacred Heart,
for All Once Broken
98 98

O sacred heart, for all once broken,
your precious Blood for sinners shed,
those words of love by you were spoken
that raised to life the living dead!

O heart, your love for all outpouring
in pain upon the cross you bled;
come now with life, our life restoring,
O heart by which our hearts are fed!

Text: James Quinn, SJ, ©.
Possible Tunes: ST. CLEMENT (98 98);
    RENDEZ Á DIEU (98 98D)
Topics: Benediction, Blood of Christ, Communion, Real Presence

Jesus' Body,
Here We Greet You

Jesus' body, here we greet you,
virgin-born of David's line,
Paschal victim, giv'n to save us
under forms of bread and wine,
body broken, life-blood flowing,
water streaming, from wounded side:
risen body, when we journey
home from exile, be our guide!
Way of truth, lead us!
Bread of life, feed us!
Mary's Son, show us your mercy!

Text: *Ave, verum corpus natum*, 14th cent.;
    trans. by James Quinn, SJ, ©.
Topics: Benediction, Body of Christ, Blood of Christ, Communion

King, in This Gift of Bread
66 66 with refrain

Response
King, from our hands receive
these gifts of your giving.

King, in this gift of bread
receive the world's homage.
See in this gift of wine
the joy of creation.

Take to your Father's throne
our hearts' true devotion.
Give from your royal hands
your Kingdom of glory.

Give for the sinful world
your flesh in atonement,
shedding your life-blood, Lord,
in mystic oblation.

Give us yourself as Food,
give life from this chalice.
So shall we eat and drink
the joy of salvation.

Text: James Quinn, SJ, ©.
Topics: Communion, Salvation

66

Zion, Sing in Exultation
887 887

Zion, sing in exultation,
sing your song of jubilation,
sing in praise of Christ, your King.
Sing to Christ in adoration,
sing the new song of salvation,
homage to your Savior bring.

Sing of love beyond all telling,
love from Jesus' heart upwelling,
giving all that love can give.
See him as his life is ending,
to his chosen friends attending,
giving all that all might live.

Greet your Lord with acclamation,
sing with joy in celebration
of his gift of living bread.
Let your mind with love be dwelling
on his gift, all gifts excelling,
gift by which your heart is fed.

See the King his table spreading;
see the Lamb his lifeblood shedding;
see in blood the New Law sealed.
All is new, the old has vanished;
all is real, with shadows banished,
what was hidden stands revealed.

Listen, Christ's own words obeying,
hear him now command you, saying:
"Do this in my memory."
gifts now offer, love expressing,
faith now bring, his presence blessing,
where no human eye can see.

Christians, let your faith grow stronger:
what was bread is bread no longer;
blood is here where once was wine.
Touch and sight are here deceivers,
mind and heart, be true believers:
truth is here beneath the sign.

Bread and wine are here concealing
what to faith God is revealing:
outward signs his glory hide.
Bread becomes its very Giver,
wine redemption's mighty river,
flowing from the Savior's side.

When we eat the bread of gladness,
there is here no cause for sadness:
Christ can suffer pain no more.
One or many, each is given
whole, entire, the bread of heaven:
mortal minds can but adore.

Bad and good, in equal measure,
find the selfsame hidden treasure,
with unequal loss and gain.
Here the good receive salvation,
sinners earn their condemnation:
from one table, joy or pain.

When you see the host divided,
let your faith by this be guided:
ev'ry fragment Christ contains.
Risen body is not broken,
only outward sign and token:
Christ his living self remains.

Praise to Jesus, bread from heaven,
angel's food to pilgrims given,
seal of peace on sin forgiven,
God the Father's gift of love.
In one perfect immolation
see fulfilled for all creation
Isaac's off'ring, lamb's oblation,
manna raining from above.

Text: *Lauda, Sion, Salvatorem* by St. Thomas
Aquinas; trans. by James Quinn, SJ, ©.
Topics: Benediction, Communion, Maundy Thursday,
Music, Real Presence

Now Let All on Earth Fall Silent

87 87 87

Now let all on earth fall silent,
bending low in holy fear;
let all hearts to heav'n be lifted
from the world of shadows here,
for the King of kings in splendor
to his altar-throne draws near.

Christ our God, the Lord of glory,
comes to be our heav'nly Bread;
he will give to us his lifeblood
who for us his lifeblood shed,
he the Priest and he the Victim,
he the meal before us spread.

Choirs of angels gather round us,
dominations, powers on high,
Cherubs, seraphs, bowed in homage;
"Alleluia, alleluia,
alleluia, God is nigh."

Text: *Liturgy of St. James*, 5th cent.;
     trans. by James Quinn, SJ, ©.
Possible Tune: PICARDY
Topics: Communion, Offertory

May Flights of Angels Lead You on Your Way

10 10 10 10 10 10

May God the Father look on you with love,
and call you to himself in bliss above.
May God the Son, good Shepherd of his sheep,
stretch out his hand and waken you from sleep.
May God the Spirit breathe on you his peace,
where joys beyond all knowing never cease.

May flights of angels lead you on your way
to paradise and heaven's eternal day!
May martyrs greet you after death's dark night,
and bid you enter into Zion's light!
May choirs of angels sing you to your rest
with once poor Lazarus, now for ever blest!

Your Body, Jesus, Once for Us Was Broken

11 10 11 10

Your Body, Jesus, once for us was broken,
your Blood outpoured to heal a wounded world.
You rose from death in glory of the Spirit,
your royal flag victoriously unfurled.

So now these signs of Bread and Wine, re-telling
your dying gift, your living self proclaim.
Until you come in splendor at earth's ending
your people, Lord, your hidden presence here
     acclaim.

Text: *In paradisum*, from the Funeral Rite;
     trans. by James Quinn, SJ, ©.
Possible Tune: SONG 1
Topics: Death, Funerals

Text: James Quinn, SJ, ©.
Topics: Blood of Christ, Body of Christ, Communion

Remember Those, O Lord
SM

Remember those, O Lord,
who in your peace have died,
yet may not gain love's high reward
till love is purified!

With you they faced death's night,
sealed with your victory sign,
soon may the splendor of your light
on them for ever shine!

Sweet is their pain, yet deep,
till perfect love is born;
their lone night-watch they gladly keep
before your radiant morn!

Your love is their great joy;
your will their one desire;
as finest gold without alloy
refine them in love's fire!

For them we humbly pray:
perfect them in your love!
O may we share eternal day
with them in heaven above!

Out of the Depths of Love
66 66 44 44

Out of the depths of love
my song to thee I sing:
I long for bliss above
with thee, my Lord and King!
Yet lovingly
I wait until
it is thy will
to gaze on me!

With flame of love on fire,
yet is my soul at rest:
thou art my heart's desire,
what thou dost will is best!
However long
my exile be,
I trust in thee,
who art my song!

Deeply I feel love's pain,
yet is love's burden light:
thou dost my soul sustain
who art my whole delight!
Thou art my peace;
through darkest days
my song of praise
shall never cease!

With wounds of love so sweet
thou dost prepare my heart
to love thee as is meet,
to know thee as thou art!
So will I sing
my song of love
in heaven above
to thee, my King!

Text: James Quinn, SJ, ©.
Possible Tune: FRANCONIA
Topics: Death, Funerals, New Heaven

Text: James Quinn, SJ, ©.
Possible Tune: LOVE UNKNOWN
Topics: Funerals, Holy Souls, Mary

A Voice Spoke from Heav'n
55 55

A voice spoke from heav'n,
"Write down what I say:
how favored are those
who die in the Lord!"

The Spirit says this:
"How favored they are,
whose work is now done,
whose good deeds remain!"

Text: James Quinn, SJ, ©.
Scripture Reference: Revelations 14:13
Topics: Death, Funerals

How Loving and Patient Is God
CM with refrain

Response
Give rest to your servants, O Lord,
who have died in your peace.

How loving and patient is God,
and how gracious to all;
how slow to remember our sins,
and how quick to forgive.

The Lord looks with love on his friends,
who revere him as God.
His justice is steadfast and true,
everlasting his love.

All ages will share in his peace
if they serve him in truth,
obeying his will in their heart,
keeping faith with is law.

How Gracious Is God
96 96 with refrain

Response
I sing of your goodness forever
in the land of the free.

How gracious is God, and how loving
in his pity for all.
He stretches his hand to the helpless,
to myself in my need.

I trusted in God, though I told him:
"I am deeply distressed."
I trusted, yet cried in my anguish:
"There is none that I can trust."

How precious the death of his loved ones
in the eyes of the Lord.
O Lord, I will serve you for ever;
for your love sets me free.

Text: James Quinn, SJ, ©.
Topics: Funerals

Text: Psalm 103 (102):8-10, 17-18; para. by
James Quinn, SJ, ©.
Topics: Death, Funeral

Praise the Lord, All You Nations
77 77

Praise the Lord, all you nations,
praise the Lord, all you peoples:
we have witnessed his mercy,
he is faithful for ever.

Praise the Father, who made us,
praise his Son, who redeemed us,
praise their life-giving Spirit,
praise one God through all ages.

Response (for funerals)
    May the angels go with you
    to the home of God's glory;
    may the saints bid you welcome
    to the land of the living.
or
    I shall go to God's temple,
    where the angels adore him;
    I shall go to his dwelling,
    and rejoice in his presence.

Remember, Father, Loving Lord
LM

Remember, Father, loving Lord,
all who at peace with you have died,
yet may not gain love's high reward
till love by Love is purified.

With Christ their King they faced death's night,
their strength his cross, our vict'ry sign;
soon may the splendor of his light
in heav'nly glory round them shine.

In peace they wait as love grows deep
till perfect love at last is born;
their lone night-watch they gladly keep
before the radiant light of morn.

Love is their pain; love is their joy;
love is their hope, their one desire.
Make them as gold without alloy,
refined in Love's consuming fire.

For them in simple trust we pray:
show them the vision of your love;
grant that we all may share that day
of endless joy in heav'n above.

We praise you, Father, fount of love;
we praise you, Christ, for vict'ry won;
we praise you, Spirit, peaceful Dove;
we praise you, God, for ever one.

Text: James Quinn, SJ, ©.
Scripture Reference: Psalm 116
Topics: Praise, Funerals, Trinity

Text: James Quinn, SJ, ©.
Possible Tune: ANGELUS (SONG 34)
Topics: Death, Funerals, New Heaven

Christ Be Beside Me
555 4D

Christ be beside me,
Christ be before me,
Christ be behind me,
King of my heart.
Christ be within me,
Christ be below me,
Christ be above me,
never to part.

Christ on my right hand,
Christ on my left hand,
Christ all around me,
Shield in the strife.
Christ in my sleeping,
Christ in my sitting,
Christ in my rising,
Light of my life.

Christ be in all hearts
thinking about me,
Christ be on all tongues
telling of me.
Christ be the vision
in eyes that see me,
in ears that hear me
Christ ever be.

We Praise You, God, Confessing You As Lord
10 10 10 10 10 10

We praise you, God, confessing you as Lord!
eternal Father, all earth worships you!
Angelic choirs, high heavens, celestial powers,
cherubs and seraphs praise you ceaselessly:
"All-holy Lord, O God of heavenly hosts,
your glorious majesty fills heaven and earth!"

Blessed apostles join in praise of you
with prophets famed and martyrs clothed in white,
singing with Holy Church throughout the earth:
"Father, we praise your boundless majesty!
We praise your glorious, true and only Son!
We praise you, Holy Spirit, Paraclete!"

You are the King of glory, Jesus Christ!
You are the Father's everlasting Son!
Born for us all from lowly Virgin's womb,
death you have conquered, opening heaven to faith!
Throned now in glory at the Father's side,
you shall return, faith teaches, as our judge!

We pray you, therefore, give your servants aid
whom you have ransomed with your precious Blood!
Let them be ranked in glory with your saints!
Save, Lord, the people who are wholly yours!
Bless them, for they are your inheritance,
and, as their ruler, ever raise them up!

Throughout each single day we bless you, Lord;
for all eternity we praise your name!
Keep us this day, Lord, free from every sin!
Have mercy on us, Lord; have mercy, Lord!
Show us your love, as we have hoped in you!
You are my hope, Lord! You shall fail me not!

Text: Adapt. from *St. Patrick's Breastplate* (8th cent.)
  by James Quinn, SJ, ©.
Possible Tunes: BUNESSAN, MANY MANSIONS (Cutts)
Topics: Christian Life, Close of Worship, Comfort and
  Encouragement, Guidance, King (Christ as),
  Recessional, Witness

Text: *Te deum*, ascribed to St. Nicetas (c. 335); trans.
  by James Quinn, SJ, ©.
Possible Tune: SONG 1
Topics: Close of Worship, Praise, Recessional,
  Thanksgiving

Forth in the Peace of Christ We Go
LM

Forth in the peace of Christ we go;
Christ to the world with joy we bring;
Christ in our minds, Christ on our lips,
Christ in our hearts, the world's true King.

King of our hearts, Christ makes us kings;
kingship with him, his servants gain;
with Christ, the Servant-Lord of all,
Christ's world we serve to share Christ's reign.

Priests of the world, Christ sends us forth
this world of time to consecrate,
our world of sin by grace to heal,
Christ's world in Christ to re-create.

Prophets of Christ, we hear his Word:
he claims our minds, to search his ways;
he claims our lips, to speak his truth;
he claims our hearts, to sing his praise.

We are his Church, he makes us one:
here is one hearth for all to find;
here is one flock, one Shepherd-King;
here is one faith, one heart, one mind.

Text: James Quinn, SJ, 1969, 1987, ©.
Possible Tunes: ANGELUS, DUKE STREET, LLEDROD
Topics: Close of Worship, Love (for others), Ministry
    and Service, Missions, Recessional, Witness

O Priest and Victim, Lord of Life
LM

O Priest and Victim, Lord of life,
throw wide the gates of paradise!
we face our foes in mortal strife;
You are our strength: O heed our cries!

To Father, Son, and Spirit blest,
one only God, be ceaseless praise!
May he in goodness grant us rest
in heav'n, our home, for endless days!

Text: *O salutaris,* Thomas Aquinas (1227-74); trans.
    by James Quinn, SJ, ©.
Possible Tune: MELCOMBE
Topics: Benediction, Enemies

See "Forth from on High the Father Sends" (*Verbum supernum*)

Come Adore This Wondrous Presence
87 87 87

Come adore this wondrous presence,
bow to Christ, the source of grace.
Here is kept the ancient promise
of God's earthly dwelling-place.
Sight is blind before God's glory,
faith alone may see his face.

Glory be to God the Father,
praise to his coequal Son,
adoration to the Spirit,
bond of love, in Godhead one.
Blest be God by all creation
joyously while ages run. Amen.

Text: *Tantum ergo,* St. Thomas Aquinas (1227-74);
    trans. by James Quinn, SJ, ©.
Possible Tune: ST. THOMAS
Topics: Benediction, Maundy Thursday, Praise

See also "Hail Our Savior's Glorious Body"

Mass Verses for Adults
11 11 11 5

Processional
God's holy people, gathered in his presence,
come to renew his covenant of mercy,
made in the life-blood of our paschal victim,
Jesus, our Savior.

Gospel
Life-giving Word, come down to save your people;
open our minds to know what you would teach us;
grow in our hearts, O seed of heaven's harvest;
be our true wisdom.

Word of the Father, be the word that saves us;
lamp to our footsteps, scatter all our darkness;
sword of the spirit, Word of God, protect us;
be our salvation.

Offertory
Father, accept this spotless bread, this chalice;
these are the gifts your grateful children offer;
with them we give ourselves to be for ever
yours and yours only.

Spirit of Jesus, rest upon this altar,
changing this bread to be his sacred body,
making this chalice flow with our salvation,
life-blood of Jesus.

Pilgrims, we hunger for the bread from heaven;
Jesus, our manna, come again among us,
giving yourself, one food for all who love you,
feeding one body.

Communion
Silent he lies, the Lord upon his altar,
Jesus, God's Lamb, whose blood is our salvation,
come to renew his covenant of glory
now and for ever.

Here we are fed at God the Father's table;
here we are one with him and with each other;
here is the promise of delight unending,
foretaste of heaven.

Recessional
Praise to the Father, who provides this banquet;
praise to the Son, who feeds us with his Body;
praise to the Spirit, bond of love, who makes us
one in one Body.

Text: James Quinn, SJ, ©.
Possible Tune: HERR DEINEN ZORN

Mass Verses for Children
11 11 11 5

Processional
Father in heaven, smile upon your children.
We are your family, gathered here to praise you.
Jesus, our Brother, teaches us to call you
dearest of fathers.

Gospel
Standing in silence, now we hear God's Gospel.
Jesus is with us, telling us of heaven.
Jesus, our Teacher, speak, for we are listening.
Welcome, Lord Jesus.

Offertory
Come, holy Spirit, bless the gifts we offer.
Change this pure bread and make it Jesus' Body.
Change this pure wine to be the Blood of Jesus.
Bless all here present.

Communion
Father, we thank you for the food you give us.
Jesus, true Bread, we welcome you among us.
Spirit of love, make all of us one Body,
loving each other.

Recessional
Praised be the Father, who has given us Jesus.
Praised be his Son, who feeds us with his Body.
Praised be the Spirit, sent by Son and Father,
making us holy.

Text: James Quinn, SJ, ©.
Possible Tune: HERR DEINEN ZORN
Topics: Children

Word of God, Come Down on Earth

78 78 88

Word of God, come down on earth,
living rain from heav'n descending;
touch our hearts and bring to birth
faith and hope and love unending.
Word almighty, we revere you;
Word made flesh, we long to hear you.

Word eternal, throned on high,
Word that brought to life creation,
Word that came from heav'n to die,
crucified for our salvation,
saving Word, the world restoring,
speak to us, your love outpouring.

Word that caused blind eyes to see,
speak and heal our mortal blindness;
deaf we are; our healer be;
loose our tongues to tell your kindness.
Be our Word in pity spoken,
heal the world, by our sin broken.

Word that speaks your Father's love,
one with him beyond all telling,
Word that sends us from above
God the Spirit, with us dwelling;
Word of truth, to all truth lead us;
Word of life, with one Bread feed us.

Text: James Quinn, SJ, ©.
Possible Tune: LIEBSTER JESU
Scripture References: st. 1: Isaiah 55:10-11;
    st. 2: John 1:1-18; st. 4: John 6
Topics: Christmas, Communion, Word of God

Alleluia, Alleluia

Refrain
Lord, speak your words of peace,
inspiring your people.

Alleluia, alleluia,
Wisdom, enthroned on high,
be our light to our darkness.
Open our hearts to hear
your word of salvation.
    Refrain
Alleluia, alleluia.

Alleluia, alleluia.
King, speak the law of love
that rules in your kingdom.
This is your one command:
to love one another.
    Refrain
Alleluia, alleluia.

Alleluia, alleluia.
Yours is the word of life,
O Word of the Father.
Sower of heav'nly seed,
sow peace and true freedom.
    Refrain
Alleluia, alleluia.

O Light from Light

LM

O Light from Light, our footsteps guide!
O living Word, our wisdom be!
O loving Heart, our hearts inspire!
Speak, O Lord! Your servants hear!

Text: James Quinn, SJ, ©.
Possible Tune: O LIGHT FROM LIGHT
Topics: Gospel verse, Light, Word of God

Text: James Quinn, SJ, ©.
Topics: Alleluias, Peace (World), Word of God

I Am the Word That Spoke and Light Was Made
10 10 10 10

I am the Word that spoke and light was made;
I am the seed that died to be re-born;
I am the bread that comes from heav'n above;
I am the vine that fills your cup with joy.

I am the way that leads the exile home;
I am the truth that sets the captive free;
I am the life that raises up the dead;
I am your peace, true peace my gift to you.

I am the Lamb that takes away your sin;
I am the gate that guards you night and day;
You are my flock: you know the shepherd's voice;
You are my own: your ransom is my blood.

Text: James Quinn, SJ, ©.
Possible Tune: STONELAW, SONG 24
Topics: Communion, Lamb of God, Light, Word of God

Pax verses
Peace with the Father
10 10

Peace with the Father, peace with Christ his Son,
peace with the Spirit, keep us ever one.

Love of the Father, love of Christ his Son,
love of the Spirit, make all Christians one.

Sin has divided those whom Christ made one;
Father, forgive us through your loving Son.

Send forth your Spirit, Father, from above
on us, your children, one with Christ in love.

Christians, forgive each other from your heart;
Christ be among us, nevermore to part.

Text: James Quinn, SJ, ©.
Possible Tune: SONG 46
Topics: Love of God, Peace, Unity

Day Is Done
84 84 88 84

Day is done, but Love unfailing
dwells ever here;
shadows fall,. but hope, prevailing,
calms every fear.
Loving Father, none forsaking,
take our hearts, of Love's own making,
watch our sleeping, guard our waking,
be always near!

Dark descends, but Light unending
shines through our night;
you are with us, ever lending
new strength to sight;
one in love, your truth confessing,
one in hope of heaven's blessing,
may we see, in love's possessing,
love's endless light!

Eyes will close, but you, unsleeping,
watch by our side;
death may come: in Love's safe keeping
still we abide.
God of love, all evil quelling,
sin forgiving, fear dispelling,
stay with us, our hearts indwelling,
this eventide!

Text: James Quinn, SJ, ©.
Possible Tune: AR HYD Y NOS
Topics: Close of worship, Evening, Light,
    Love (God's to us), Recessional

Now Fades All Earthly Splendor
76 76 766

Now fades all earthly splendor;
the shades of night descend;
the dying of the daylight
foretells creation's end.
Though noon gives place to sunset,
yet dark gives place to light;
with dawn's new hope is bright.

The silver notes of morning
will greet the rising sun,
as once the Easter glory
shone round the Risen One.
So will the night of dying
give place to heaven's day,
and hope of heaven's vision
will light our pilgrim way.

So will the new creation
rise from the old re-born
to splendor in Christ's glory
and everlasting morn.
All darkness will be ended
as faith gives place to sight
of Father, Son, and Spirit,
one God, in heaven's light.

Light of Undying Glory, Shine
LM

Light of undying glory, shine,
warming our hearts with love divine;
come from the gracious Father's side,
bathe us in joy this eventide.

Lord Jesus Christ, your living breath
restores the world from sin and death;
giver of life and Lord of grace,
show us the splendor of your face.

Westward the sun is lost to sight,
the star of ev'ning marks the night;
be, Lord, the lamp that shed the glow
of heaven's radiance here below.

All-holy Father, only Son,
spirit of love, for ever one,
let all the world its voice now raise
to sing your everlasting praise.

Text: James Quinn, SJ, ©.
Possible Tune: EWING, CRUGER
Scripture Reference: Ephesians 6:10-17
Topics: Evening, Light

Text: *Phos hilaron,* 3rd cent. or earlier;
  trans. by James Quinn, SJ, ©.
Possible Tunes: SONG 5, ANGELUS
Topics: Evening, Light

Now at the Daylight's Ending
76 76

Now at the daylight's ending
we turn, O God, to you:
send forth your Holy Spirit;
our spirit now renew.
To you in adoration,
in thankfulness and praise,
in faith and hope and gladness,
our loving hearts we raise.

The gift you gave at daylight
this night you take away,
to leave within our keeping
the blessings of this day.

Take all its joy and sorrow;
take all that love can give;
but all that needs forgiveness,
dear Father, now forgive.

With watchful eyes, O shepherd,
look down upon your sheep;
stretch forth your hands in healing
and close our eyes in sleep.

Come down, O Holy Spirit,
to be our loving Guest;
be near us, holy angels,
and guard us as we rest.

We praise you, heav'nly Father:
from you all light descends;
you give us heaven's glory
when life's brief daylight ends.

We praise you, Jesus, Savior,
the light of heav'n above;
we praise you, Holy Spirit,
the living flame of love.

Darkness Has Faded, Night Gives Way to Morning
11 11 11 5

Darkness has faded, night gives way to morning;
sleep has refreshed us, now we thank our Maker,
singing his praises, lifting up to heaven
hearts, minds, and voices.

Father of mercies, bless the hours before us;
while there is daylight may we work to please you,
building a city fit to be your dwelling,
home for all nations.

Daystar of heaven, dawn that ends our darkness,
sun of salvation, Lord enthroned in splendor,
stay with us, Jesus; let your Easter glory
fill all creation.

Flame of the Spirit, fire with love's devotion
hearts that are lukewarm; make us true apostles;
give us a vision wide as heav'n's horizon,
bright with your promise.

Father in heaven, guide your children homewards;
Jesus our Brother, walk beside us always;
joy-giving Spirit, make the world one people,
sign of God's Kingdom.

Text: James Quinn, SJ, ©.
Possible Tune: CHRISTUS DER IST MEIN LEBEN
Topics: Evening, Light, Praise and Adoration,
    Thanksgiving

Text: James Quinn, SJ, ©.
Possible Tune: DIVA SERVATRIX
Scripture Reference: John 9:4, Rev. 22:16, Acts 2:1-4
Topics: Holy Spirit, Morning, Thanksgiving

O God of Light, the Dawning Day
LM

O God of light, the dawning day
gives us new promise of your love;
each fresh beginning is your gift,
like gentle dew from heav'n above.

Your blessings, Father, never fail:
your Son, who is our daily Bread,
the Holy Spirit of your love,
by whom each day our hearts are led.

Make us the servants of your peace,
renew our strength, remove all fear;
be with us, Lord, throughout this day,
for all is joy if you are near.

To Father, Son, and Spirit blest,
one only God, we humbly pray:
show us the splendor of your light
in death, the dawn of perfect day.

First of All Days, New-Born
Irregular with refrain

Refrain
Holy day of the Lord,
all ages rejoice in your glory!
This is the day God made,
day of our peace and our joy!

First of all days, new-born
when God's Word spoke in the darkness:
Light came to be at your birth,
dawn of a noonday to come!
    Refrain

Day of a world made whole,
you saw Christ rising in splendor!
He is our day without end,
he is our light and our life!
    Refrain

Day of God's gift restored,
you saw God's Spirit descending!
Spirit of love and of truth,
give us your warmth and your light!
    Refrain

Text: *Salve festa Dies*, Venantius Honorius Fortunatus
(ca. 540-600); trans. by James Quinn, SJ, ©.
Possible Tune: SALVE FESTA DIES
Topics: Christmas, Easter, Morning, Light, Lord's Day,
    Pentecost

Text: James Quinn, SJ, ©.
Possible Tune: DANBY
Topics: Christian Life, Morning

My Jesus, My Love, Look with Pity on Me

11 9 11 9D

My Jesus, my love, look with pity on me,
for whose sake you breathed forth your last breath.
I think of the wounds in your hands and your feet,
and the heart that was pierced after death.
I bless the rich stream that has washed me from sin
in your blood and the water of grace.
When death comes, I pray, take me home to your side,
to rejoice as I gaze on your face.

I think on my past, when I caused you such pain:
touch my heart with true sorrow and shame.
Grant time for repentance, for making amends:
you are Jesus; I call on your name.
The angels of heav'n take delight when they see
the lost sheep carried back to the flock.
When Peter disowned you, you welcomed him back
to be shepherd, apostle, and rock.

O Mary, my Mother, protect me from harm;
wrap me round in your mantle of blue.
You stood by your Son in compassion and love,
when he gave us as children to you.
O Mother of Jesus, our Savior and God,
be our Mother to bring us re-birth;
you now share his glory in heaven above,
look with love on your children on earth.

Text: James Quinn, SJ, 1990, ©. Adapted from the
    Gaelic of John Hoare, a Munster poet of the 18th
    cent.
Possible Tune:
Topics: Confession of Sin, Forgiveness, Guidance, Lent,
    Mary, Repentance, Suffering of Christ

Hymns for the Church in the World

Be in My Seeing
10 10 10 10

Be in my seeing,
O God of my heart:
all is as nothing
beside heaven's King.
Be in my thinking
by day and by night.
Be in my sleeping,
the dream of my soul.

Be in my speaking;
be light of my mind.
Be, Lord, within me;
may I be in you.
Be my dear Father;
may I be your child.
Be my own always;
take me as your own.

Be, Lord, my war-shield,
the sword in my hand.
Be my high honor;
be all my delight.
Be my protection,
my fortress of strength.
Bring me where angels
are singing your praise.

Be my salvation
in body and soul.
Be my true kingdom
in heav'n and on earth.
Be my own loved one,
great joy of my heart,
You and no other,
O heaven's high King.

Text: James Quinn, SJ, ©.
Source: *Rob tu mo bhoile*
Possible Tune: BE THOU MY VISION
Topics: Christian Life, Guidance, Illumination, Opening
    of Worship, Processional

Christ Our God Is Here Among Us, As He Promised

12 12 12 12 with refrain

God is love, and where true love is, God himself
is there.

Christ our God is here among us, as he promised.
Christ has loved us, Christ has called us, Christ is
  with us.
Full of gladness, let us welcome Christ our brother.
Let us see him, let us love him, in our neighbor.

God is love, and where true love is, God himself
is there.

God has made us one to love him, one to praise him.
Let our minds be pure and holy, one with Jesus.
Let our hearts be full of kindness, full of mercy.
Let our words be words of friendship, words of
  blessing.

God is love, and where true love is, God himself
is there.

Loving Jesus, stay beside us, now and always.
King and Shepherd, take us with you home to
  heaven.
God and Savior, may we praise you with the angels.
Lord of glory, may we see you, throned in splendor.

Christians, Your Call Is from God

78 78 with refrain

Response
Christians, your life is to love,
for Christ has made you one Body.

Christians, your call is from God,
in Christ live up to your calling:
bear with each other in love,
be humble, gentle and patient.

Christians, as Christ made you one
by giving life in the Spirit,
so in the bond of his peace
be always one in his Spirit.

One is the Body of Christ,
one Spirit dwells in that Body,
one is the glorious hope
to which the Father has called you.

Yours is one Lord, and one faith,
one birth by water and Spirit;
yours is one Father of all,
above all, through all and in all.

Text: *Ubi Caritas est Vera,* Latin, 9th cent.;
    trans. by James Quinn, SJ, ©.
Possible Tune: UBI CARITAS EST VERA
Topics: Maundy Thursday, Presence (God's), Praise

Text: James Quinn, SJ, ©.
Topics: Christian Life, Unity

Eternal God in Trinity
LM

Eternal God in Trinity,
whose name is Love, you made our race
to share your life, that you might reign
in one communion, born of grace.

Christ's sinless Mother, for his sake
God chose you as his dwelling-place,
that fitting shrine in which he lay
until at last you saw his face.

Lord Jesus Christ, true God, true man,
you rose from death as sov'reign Lord,
God's First-born Son, creation's King,
to share with us your great reward.

Lord God, we thank you for your Church:
you sent your Spirit to inspire
our loveless hearts, to make all one
with love re-born in tongues of fire.

My master, Francis, sing your song
that pierced my heart with joy and pain;
let all creation hear your voice,
and learn from you when loss is gain.

Great God of love, of joy, of peace,
yours is the gift of unity;
teach us to find our truest selves
in you, one God in Trinity.

God of Truth
66 76

Refrain
Glorify, magnify,
bless the Lord, sing for joy!
Alleluia, praise his name!
Give him thanks evermore!

God of truth, take our minds,
God of grace, take our souls,
God most holy, take our wills,
God of love, take our hearts.

Son of God, come to save,
Son of man, come as judge,
Son of Mary, come in love,
Servant-Son, come as priest.

Gift of God, give us faith,
Lord of life, give us hope,
Holy Spirit, give us love,
bond of love, make us one.

Lord of lords, be our peace,
King of kings, be our life,
bliss eternal, be our joy,
mighty God, be our all.

Text: James Quinn, SJ, 1988, ©.
Possible Tune: GOD OF TRUTH
Topics: Offering, Praise and Adoration, Prayer,
     Thanksgiving

Text: James Quinn, SJ, 1991, ©.
Possible Tune: O WALY, WALY
Topics: Church, Trinity

Lord God, You Made Us for Yourself

LM

Lord God, you made us for yourself,
to love and serve you in your Son.
He is the way that leads to life,
his glory and our joy are one.

All that you made is gift and grace,
by which you raise us up to you:
help us to know what is your will,
to see the false, to choose the true.

Take from us passion, pride and greed,
give each of a heart made whole,
that we may choose the nobler way,
your greater glory, love's true goal.

Lord Jesus, Let Me Know Who You Are

10 10 10 10 10 10

Lord Jesus, let me know who you are,
and let me know myself as you know me.
Let me have no desire except for you,
let me look down on self, and love but you.
Let me do all for you, and you alone,
let me be humble by exalting you.

Let me not think of anything but you,
let me be dead to self, to live in you.
Let me receive as from your loving hands
all that life brings to me of pain and joy.
Let me say No to self but Yes to you,
and daily choose to follow where you lead.

Let me keep far from self but close to you,
that I may find my refuge in your love.
Let me fear self, and fear to lose your love,
that I may be among your chosen friends,
Let me not trust myself but trust in you,
let me obey with joy when you command.

Let me be swayed by nothing but by you,
let me be poor, to be enriched by you.
Show me your face, that I may love you more;
call me, that I may see your as you are.
Lord Jesus, let me share your joy in heav'n,
that I may be with you for evermore.

Text: James Quinn, SJ, 1989, ©.
Source: St. Ignatius Loyola
Topics: Christian Life, Creation and Providence,
    Incarnation

Text: James Quinn, SJ, ©.
Possible Tune: SONG 1
Topics: Christian Life, Offering

Lord Jesus, Let Me Live for You
LM

Lord Jesus, let me live for you:
let all I am be yours alone;
you are my true and lasting joy
if you will make me all your own.

You are the way to heav'n above,
your wounded heart the fount of grace;
let me embrace your cross of pain
that I may see your glorious face.

Our great high priest, your share your all
with me, of all the last and least:
let me be crucified with you,
to be like you, a victim-priest.

Your word of truth is all my joy,
to preach your love is my delight:
touch now my lips with heaven'ly fire
and raise my heart to heaven's height.

Let me poor with you who chose
to lay your heav'nly glory down:
enrich my life with poverty
that I may share your heav'nly crown.

Jesus, you gave me as her own
to her whose womb your body bore:
keep me, I pray, through Mary's prayers,
her servant-son for evermore.

Lord Jesus, Make Me Holy
75 75D

Lord Jesus, make me holy
in word and in thought.
Lord Jesus, give me wisdom
to do as I ought.
Lord Jesus, may I love you
and do what is right.
Protect me and guide me
by day and by night

Text: *A Íosa glan mo Chroíse;*
    trans. by James Quinn, SJ, 1991, ©.
Possible Tune: AN REALT (Trad. Irish)
Topics: Communion, Guidance, Sanctification

Lord, Let Me Love You More and More
LM

Lord, let me love you more and more,
my love for you a flowing tide;
you did not love with grudging heart,
but loved us all with arms spread wide.

Let me not measure love's return
but love you, Lord, with all my soul;
let my small love be lost in you,
and found once more as love made whole.

Teach me to love as Mary loved,
the Virgin-Mother of her Lord;
you shared with her your agony,
two hearts made one by sorrow's sword.

She is your Bride, the sinless Eve,
who now in glory gazes down
on us, the children of her pain:
lead us, we pray, to share her crown.

Text: James Quinn, SJ, ©.
Source: St. Norbert
Possible Tune: O WALY, WALY
Topics: Christian Life, Offering

Text: James Quinn, SJ, ©.
Possible Tune: O WALY, WALY
Topics: Grace, Love (of God), Mary

Lord, Make Us Servants of Your Peace
LM

Lord, make us servants of your peace;
where there is hate, may we sow love;
where there is hurt, may we forgive;
where there is strife, may we make one.

Where all is doubt, may we sow faith;
where all is gloom, may we sow hope;
where all is night, may we sow light;
where all is tears, may we sow joy.

Jesus, our Lord, may we not seek
to be consoled, but to console,
nor look to understanding hearts,
but look for hearts to understand.

May we not look for love's return,
but seek to love unselfishly,
for in our giving we receive,
and in forgiving are forgiv'n.

Dying, we live, and are reborn
through death's dark night to endless day;
Lord, make us servants of your peace,
to wake at last in heaven's light.

Text: James Quinn, SJ, based on a prayer of St. Francis
   of Assisi.
Possible Tunes: O WALY, WALY; ROCHESTER (White);
   YOUNG (Scott); DICKINSON COLLEGE (Bristol)
Topics: Christian Life, Faith, Love (for others), Ministry
   and Service, Missions, Peace (for the world), Unity,
   Witness

Love Is of God, in Love His Love Is Known
10 10

Love is of God; in love his love is known;
in those who love, the love of God is shown.

Joy is of God, in whom all joy is found;
in Christ our joy the joys of heav'n abound.

Peace is of God; like gentlest dew he sends
his peace on those whom love has made his
   friends.

Light is of God; whoever walks in light
has Christ beside him through the darkest night.

Glory is theirs in whom the Spirit dwells,
whose light all light, whose love all love excels.

Love is of God; in love his love is known;
in those who love the love of God is shown.

Text: James Quinn, SJ, ©.
Possible Tunes: SONG 46, QUINN (Fedak)
Topics: Christian Life, Communion, Joy, Light, Love
   (God's to us), Marriage, Peace (Inner)

My Freedom, Lord, My Memory
LM

My freedom, Lord, my memory,
my understanding and my will,
all that I am, all that I have,
take now and keep, to serve you still.

I freely give for you to own
your gifts to me, so freely giv'n:
take them but leave within my heart
your love, your grace, my hope of heav'n.

Text: St. Ignatius Loyola;
   trans. by James Quinn, SJ, 1989, ©.
Topics: Offering

Sing, All the World, in Praise
66 66 with refrain

Response
Glory to Christ our King,
high Priest and true Prophet.

Sing all the world, in praise
of Christ and his Kingship.
Sing to the Lord of lords,
high King of creation.

King of our hearts, O Christ,
in you is our gladness.
Give to our restless hearts
the peace of your presence.

Teach us to find your peace
in finding each other.
Those with no thought of self
are kings in your Kingdom.

Rule in our hearts, O King,
through love for each other.
Share with your servants, Lord,
your Kingship of service.

Text: James Quinn, SJ, ©.
Topics: King (Christ as), Ministry and Service,
    Peace (inner), Praise and Adoration

Bless the Lord of the Sunrise
76 76 76D

Bless the Lord of the sunrise,
    Bless the Lord of the light,
Bless the Lord of the sunset,
    Bless the Lord of the night.
Bless the Lord of the ocean,
    Bless the Lord of the sky,
Bless the Lord of the mountains,
    Bless the Lord throned on high.
Bless the Lord of the seedbed,
    Bless the Lord of the rain,
Bless the Lord of the harvest,
    Bless the Lord of the grain.

Bless the Lord of creation,
    Bless the Lord in this place,
Bless the Lord for his blessings,
    Bless the Lord for his grace.
Bless the Lord who is Shepherd,
    Bless his Body, our Bread,
Bless the Lord, our Redeemer,
    Bless his Blood, freely shed.
Bless the love of the Father,
    Bless the grace of his Son,
Bless the peace of their Spirit,
    Bless the Lord, ever One.

Teach Me To Serve You As I Should
LM

Teach me to serve you as I should,
to give my all ungrudgingly,
to fight and not to heed the wounds
but work for you untiringly.

Teach me to spend myself for you,
to ask not more as my reward
than that I know I do your will,
Jesus, my Savior and my Lord.

Text: James Quinn, SJ, 1989, ©.
Source: St. Ignatius Loyola
Topics: Christian Life, Ministry and Service

Text: James Quinn, SJ, ©.
Possible Tune: LOVELY THE WORLD
Topics: Creation, Praise, Thanksgiving

The Seed Is Christ's
88

The seed is Christ's,
the harvest his:
may we be stored
within God's barn.

The sea is Christ's,
the fish are his:
may we be caught
within God's net.

From birth to age,
from age to death,
enfold us, Christ,
within your arms.

Until the end,
the great re-birth,
Christ, be our joy
in Paradise.

Blessed Are You, Lord
11 12

Blessed are you, Lord, the God of our fathers:
You are worthy of praise and honor for ever.

Blessed and holy your name in its splendor:
You are worthy of praise and honor for ever.

Blessed are you in the shrine of your glory:
You are worthy of praise and honor for ever.

Blessed are you on the seat of your mercy:
You are worthy of praise and honor for ever.

Blessed are you in the depth of your wisdom:
You are worthy of praise and honor for ever.

Blessed are you on the throne of your kingdom:
You are worthy of praise and honor for ever.

Blessed are you in the vault of high heaven:
You are worthy of praise and honor for ever.

Blessed are you, Lord, the God of our fathers:
You are worthy of praise and honor for ever.

Blessed are you, Father, Son, Holy Spirit:
You are worthy of praise and honor for ever.

Blessed are you, the one God, through all ages:
You are worthy of praise and honor for ever.

Text: James Quinn, SJ, ©.
Possible Tune: SONG OF THREE YOUNG MEN
Scripture Reference: Daniel 3; Hebrews 9:3-5
Topics: Praise and Adoration

Text: James Quinn, SJ, ©.
Possible Tune: AG CRIOST AN SIOL
Topics: Christian Life, Creation, Offertory

My Love Is My God; My Life Is My Lord
10 8 11 8

My love is my God; my life is my Lord;
my light is the Lord of mercy;
my true love is Christ; my delight is his heart,
the heart of the King of Glory.

Your love is my love; your ways are my joy,
your glory and grace my gladness;
dear heart of my heart, I have left you by sin:
a sinner, I bow before you.

Your word is my love, to serve you my joy;
your Mother the star that guides me,
the Queen of the angels, of all saints above,
the Queen of the twelve apostles.

In glory she reigns, whose soul once was pierced,
the Queen of your cross and crowning;
as Queen of your love, at the hour when I die
may she be my shield and shelter.

My love is the choir that fills heav'n with song;
my love is your song-filled city;
my love is the flock that has left all for you;
my love is your might and mercy.

My love is yourself, whose blood flowed for me,
my love is your face in glory;
my Jesus, my King and my judge, be my friend,
my light, my delight, my loved one.

Praise the King of All Creation
89 8 89 8 66 4 44 8

Praise the King of all creation,
who gives his Son as our salvation,
the glorious firstborn from the dead!
Praise the Son, from heav'n descending
to give us life that knows no ending,
who comes to be our living Bread!
O Spirit, make all one
who feed on God's own Son!
Alleluia!
To Father, Son, and Spirit be
all glory giv'n eternally!

Text: *Mo ghrása mo Dhía*, Tadhg Gaelach O
  Suilleabháin (d. 1795); trans. by James Quinn, SJ, ©.
Topics: Church, Love (of God), Mary, Sacred Heart

Text: James Quinn, SJ, ©.
Possible Tune: WACHET AUF
Scripture Reference: Psalm 150
Topics: Communion, Creation, Thanksgiving, Unity

Sing to God with Gladness, All Creation
10 9 8 10 9 7

Sing to God with gladness, all creation!
Sing to God the song of God's great love!
Sing to God, who made the heavens!
Sing to God, who made the loveliness of earth!
Sing to the Lord! Sing Alleluia!
Sing to the Lord! Sing with joy!

Sing to God on high, O sun in splendor!
Sing to God on high, O silver moon!
Sing to God, O sky at dawning!
Sing to God, O starlit silence of the night!
Sing to the Lord! Sing Alleluia!
Sing to the Lord! Sing with joy!

Sing your song of glory, angel voices!
Sing your song of peace to all on earth!
Sing of peace, the heart's deep longing!
Sing of peace that comes from God and God alone!
Sing to the Lord! Sing Alleluia!
Sing to the Lord! Sing with joy!

Sing to God the Father, all creation!
Sing to God his dear and only Son!
Sing to God the loving Spirit!
Sing with joy to God, one God, for evermore!
Sing to the Lord! Sing Alleluia!
Sing to the Lord! Sing with joy!

Text: James Quinn, SJ, ©.
Possible Tune: STU MO RUN
Topics: Creation, Music, Praise, Thanksgiving

Sing, All My Being
11 10 11 10

Sing, all my being, sing to God who made you,
creation's Lord, who made you for his own,
who called you forth from nothing into being,
to find your truest self in him alone.

Sing out, my heart, your song to God who loved you,
who formed you for himself before your birth:
your only love is now that Love eternal
for whom are born all lesser loves of earth.

Rejoice, my soul, and sing of him who sought you,
who sought you ev'ry moment down the years,
who did not rest until at last you found him,
when perfect love was born from mother's tears.

Bow down, my mind, before the Word who taught
    you
that living truth which only he can teach;
how could you hope to find without his Spirit
the Word made flesh that faith alone can reach?

My spirit, sing with joy to him who won you
with beauty ever old, yet ever new:
unfailing fount of life and love and wisdom,
our hearts are restless till they rest in you.

All glory be to God, the gracious Father,
all glory be to God, his only Son,
all glory be to God, the Holy Spirit,
all glory be to God, forever one.

Text: James Quinn, SJ, 1985
Possible Tune: INTERCESSOR
Topics: Creation and Providence, Love (God's love),
    Music, Word of God

Dear Love of My Heart
56 56D

Heart of Jesus, Full of Wisdom
CMD

Dear love of my heart,
O heart of Christ, my Lord,
what treasure you leave
within my heart, O Guest!
you come to my heart,
O heart on fire with love,
and leave me your heart:
O how my heart is blest!

My heart cannot tell,
O King of angel hosts,
how great was that pain
you bore upon the cross:
so small is my heart,
so deep your wounds of love,
so precious the crown
of those you save from loss!

Your death has restored
your likeness in my heart;
your cross is my shield,
your loving heart my gain!
How sad is my heart
when I recall my sins!
How could I have loved
what gave your heart such pain?

O King of all bliss,
all glory set aside,
what heart could have known
the pain within your breast?
The wound in your side
laid bare your burning love,
and opened for all
the heart where all find rest!

Heart of Jesus, full of wisdom,
be the King of my heart.
Heart of Jesus, rich in mercy,
wash me clean, make me whole.
Heart of Jesus, meek and gentle,
be for ever my joy.
Heart of Jesus, my sure refuge,
be the strength of my soul.

Heart of Jesus, in the Garden
you were broken for me.
Heart of Jesus, at the Supper
you showed love to the end.
Heart of Jesus, blood and water,
source of life, flowed for me.
Heart of Jesus, in your glory
you still plead as my Friend.

Heart of Jesus, priest and victim,
draw me closer to you.
Heart of Jesus, I adore you
in the signs of your love.
Heart of Jesus, Son of Mary,
keep me childlike in grace.
Heart of Jesus, lead me with you
to my true home above.

Text: *Gile mo chroí*, Tadgh Gaelach O Suilleabháin
    (d. 1795); trans. by James Quinn, SJ, ©.
Possible Tune: DUAN CHROÍ ÍOSA
Topics: Life of Christ, Love of God, Sacred Heart

Text: James Quinn, SJ, 1991, ©.
Possible Tune: BÍ A ÍOSA (Trad. Irish)
Topics: Communion, Sacred Heart, Sanctification

God Is Enthroned As King
66 66 with refrain

Response
Sing to the Lord of all
your songs of rejoicing.

God is enthroned as King
in garments of glory;
firm his eternal throne,
unmoved his creation.

Ocean, give voices in praise
of God, your Creator.
Song of your surge, O sea,
is song to his glory.

Wise are his firm decrees
and faithful his promise.
Holy is God our Lord,
and holy his Temple.

Worship the King of heav'n,
the Father almighty,
one with his only Son,
and one with their Spirit.

Now Before the Throne of Heaven
87 87D

Now before the throne of heaven
numbers numberless I saw,
drawn from every tribe and nation,
every people, every tongue.
robed in white, they stood in splendor,
palms of vict'ry in their hands,
as they cried aloud: "Salvation
comes from God and Christ the Lamb."

"Who are these in snow-white garments,
through what testing have they come?"
"These have come through tribulation,
through the last and great ordeal.
now they stand, a white-robed army,
washed with blood of Christ the Lamb,
serving God within his temple,
praising him by day and night.

"He who sits enthroned in glory
dwells among them as their God;
thirst or hunger cannot reach them,
burning sun or scorching wind.
Christ the Lamb will be their shepherd,
leading them to living springs;
God will take from them all sorrow,
dry their eyes of every tear."

All in heaven sang in homage:
"Wisdom, honor, pow'r, and might,
blessing, glory, and thanksgiving
be to God eternally."
Glory be to God the Father;
glory be to Christ the Lamb;
glory be to God the Spirit,
strength of martyrs, joy of saints.

Text: James Quinn, SJ, ©.
Possible Tune: Hyfrydol
Scripture References: Revelation 7:9-17
Topics: Ascension and Reign, New Heaven and Earth,
    Return of Christ

Text: James Quinn, SJ, ©.
Topics: New Heaven and Earth

O White-Robed King of Glory
76 76D

O white-robed King of glory,
you come to seek your own;
with angel hosts around you,
you claim your altar-throne.
A hundred-thousand welcomes
we give you, God most high;
with loving hearts we greet you,
High King of earth and sky.

You come yourself to bring us
the hope of Paradise;
you come to lead us homeward
to joy beyond the skies.
You come in hidden glory
who yet will come again
in majesty and splendor
to be our great Amen.

O King of kings, in wonder
we wait for that bless'd morn,
new springtime of creation,
when all shall be reborn.
Then by your word almighty
the promised heav'n and earth
in glory and in gladness
at last shall come to birth.

Salvation Is God's
55 55 with refrain

Response
All Kingship is yours!
All glory and pow'r!

Salvation is God's
and glory and pow'r,
his judgements are true
his judgements are just!

Give praise to our God,
you servants of God,
both little and great,
revering his name.

The Lord is now King,
the ruler of all.
Give glory to him,
in him take your joy.

The wedding day dawns
for Lamb and for Bride;
in beauty adorned,
she waits for the Lamb.

The grace of the Lamb
had robed her in white;
in glory she shines,
fit Bride for the Lamb.

How happy are those
invited to share
the supper prepared
for Bridegroom and Bride!

Text: James Quinn, SJ, ©.
Possible Tune: Killin
Scripture References: Matthew 19:28,
II Corinthians 1:19-20, Revelation 1:13, 21:1
Topics: Ascension, Communion, Funerals

Text: James Quinn, SJ, ©.
Scripture Reference: Revelation 19:1, 2, 5-9.
Topics: King (Christ as), Praise and Adoration,
Salvation

Hymns for the Saints

The Angel Brought Mary the Word of the Lord
11 11 11 11

The angel brought Mary the word of the Lord:
rejoice, full of grace, for the Lord is with you.
the Spirit of God will come down in his pow'r:
the Child you will bear will be called Son of God.

Behold, said Our Lady, the handmaid of God;
may his will be done as your words have revealed.
The word became man in a body like ours,
and dwelt in our midst as God's glory on earth.

Our Lord took from Mary his body and blood;
so now may these gifts become Jesus, our King.
Our Savior will give us his body as food,
his blood as our drink, to make all of us one.

Text: James Quinn, SJ, 1991, ©.
Possible Tunes: CRADLE SONG, NORMANDY
Topics: Communion, Mary, Offertory

Gabriel, to Mary Sent
77 77 88 443 776

Gabriel, to Mary sent,
bowed low in her chaste dwelling
thus he spoke of God's intent,
his words all fear dispelling:
"Hail, Queen of virgins, God greets thee!
The Lord of sky and earth and sea
shall be thy Son,
thy darling One,
O Maiden!
Heav'n's gate now shalt thou be!
O hope of all sin-laden,
thy Son shall set them free!"

Mary pondered: "What means this?
a maid I am for ever!
Giv'n to God is mother's bliss;
God's bond I ne'er will sever!"
The angel said: "The Spirit's pow'r
shall rest on thee at this blest hour!
So do not fear!
be of good cheer,
for surely
thy spotless love shall flow'r
in God's own Son all purely,
thy virgin womb his bow'r!"

Straightway Mary made reply:
"Behold the handmaid lowly
of Almighty God on high,
whose name is ever holy!
Thou art his envoy from above,
entrusted with his plan of love!
Take my consent!
My one intent
his pleasure,
to serve him all my task!
his will is my whole treasure,
whatever he may ask!"

Thank we Mary for our Lord!
her Son we thank who saved us!
Peace with God is our reward,
where sin before enslaved us!
Dear Son of Mary, smile on those
whom thou hast saved from endless woes!
The human race
is by thy grace
forgiven!
Do thou at exile's close,
who hast for us sore striven,
grant us thy blest repose!

Text: *Angelus ad virginem*, 14th cent.; trans. by
   James Quinn, SJ, ©.
Possible Tune: ANGELUS AD VIRGINEM
Topics: Biblical names (Gabriel), Mary

Guide Us, Star of Ocean
65 65

Guide us, Star of Ocean,
shining in the sky,
God's own Virgin Mother,
geaven's gate on high!

God invites his handmaid:
peace on earth renew!
din of Eve, our mother,
dinless Eve, undo!

Touch those eyes that see not;
dlaves of sin unchain;
keep us from all evil;
nlessings for us gain!

Chosen as his Mother
by God's Holy One,
pray for us, your children,
to your Savior-Son!

Spotless Virgin Mother,
sinners we have been,
pure and gentle-hearted
make us, gracious Queen!

Keep us ever holy,
huide our steps in grace,
till we share your gladness
when we see God's face!

Praise now God the Father,
glorify his Son,
honor God the Spirit,
all in Godhead one!

Hail, Our Queen
and Mother Blest
76 76D

Hail, our Queen and Mother blest!
joy when all was sadness,
life and hope you brought to birth,
mother of our gladness!
Children of the sinful Eve,
dinless Eve, befriend us,
exiled in this vale of tears:
strength and comfort send us!

Pray for us, O Patroness,
be our consolation!
Lead us home to see your Son,
Jesus, our salvation!
Gracious are you, full of grace,
loving as none other,
joy of heaven and joy of earth,
Mary, God's own Mother!

Text: *Salve Regina*, Hermannus Contractus (d. 1054);
    trans. by James Quinn, SJ, ©.
Possible Tune: AVE, VIRGO VIRGINUM
Topics: Mary

Hail, Mary, Full of Gladness

Hail, Mary, full of gladness
at your Annunciation
when Gabriel proclaimed the Incarnation
of God's own Son and yours to banish sadness!
Hail, Mary, full of gladness!

Hail, Mary, Virgin-Mother!
What joy was yours, O Maiden,
your virgin womb with child so sweetly laden,
the dwelling of God's Son and of none other!
Hail, Mary, Virgin-Mother.

Hail, Mary, our dear Mother!
So dares the Church to name you!
our Mother we on earth may proudly claim you,
for we are one with Christ, your Son, our Brother.
Hail, Mary, our dear Mother!

Text: James Quinn, SJ, ©.
Possible Tune: MODA
Topics: Mary

Text: *Ave maris stella*, 9th cent.;
    trans. by James Quinn, SJ, ©.
Possible Tune: RICHARDSON
Topics: Mary

Holy Mary, Full of Grace, We Turn to You

Holy Mary, full of grace, we turn to you:
be our help in time of need!
Loving Mother, hear your children:
look with love and pity
on us who look to you!
You are our refuge in danger:
save us, Queen in glory;
Blessed Virgin Mary, God's holy Mother!

Text: *Sub tuum praesidium;*
    trans. by James Quinn, SJ, ©.
Topics: Mary

Joy Is Yours, Mary
10 5 10 8 49 10 9

Joy is yours, Mary, graced by God's goodness.
the Lord is with you.
Among all women you are the most blessed,
and blessed is the fruit of your womb,
Jesus, our Lord.
God's virgin Mother, holy Mary,
pray for us sinners, pray for your children,
pray for us now and at life's ending. Amen.

Text: *Ave, Maria,* trans. by James Quinn, SJ, ©.
Possible Tune: AVE MARIA
Scripture Reference: Luke 1:28, 42
Topics: Mary

Joy Fill Your Heart, O Queen Most High
LM with alleluias

Joy fill your heart, O Queen most high, alleluia!
Your Son, who in the tomb did lie, alleluia!
Has ris'n as he did prophesy, alleluia!
Pray for us, Mother, when we die, alleluia!
Alleluia, alleluia, alleluia!

Text: *Regina caeli, laetare,* 12th cent.; trans. by James
    Quinn, SJ, ©.
Possible Tune: LASST UNS ERFREUEN
Topics: Easter, Mary

Mary of Carmel, Crowned with Heaven's Glory
11 11 11 5

Mary of Carmel, crowned with heaven's glory,
look on us, Mother, as we sing your praises:
be with us always, joy of saints and angels,
joy of creation.

Here on Mount Carmel peace is all around us:
here is the garden where your children gather,
praising God's goodness, voices raised in gladness,
one with our Mother.

Come to God's mountain, all who serve Our Lady:
sing to God's glory, young and old together,
gull hearts outpouring Mary's song of worship,
thanking her Maker.

Sing to the Father, who exalts his handmaid;
sing to God's wisdom, Son who chose his Mother;
sing to their Spirit, Love that overshadowed
Mary, chaste Virgin.

Text: James Quinn, SJ, ©.
Topics: Mary

Mother of Christ, Our Hope, Our Patroness
10 10 10 10

Mother of Christ, our hope, our patroness,
star of the sea, our beacon in distress.
Guide to the shores of everlasting day
God's holy people on their pilgrim way.

Virgin, in you God made his dwelling-place;
Mother of all the living, full of grace,
blessed are you: God's word you did believe;
"Yes" on your lips undid the "No" of Eve.

Daughter of God, who bore his holy One,
dearest of all to Christ, your loving Son,
show us his face, O Mother, as on earth,
loving us all, you gave our Savior birth.

Text: *Alma Redemptoris Mater;* trans. by James
    Quinn, SJ, ©.
Possible Tune: FARLEY CASTLE
Topics: Mary

97

Mother of Jesus, Mary of Ireland

10 10 12 11 9 9

Mother of Jesus, Mary of Ireland,
come in your splendor to visit your own;
with Joseph your husband and John the Beloved
still show to your children the Lamb on his throne.
Come to us, Mother, come without fail,
joy of Cnoc Mhuire, joy of the Gael!

Husband of Mary, guardian of Jesus,
save us in danger, our patron and friend;
with Mary our Mother watch over her children,
bring hope to life's journey, bring peace at its end.
Saint of the dying, conquer our fear,
give us your courage, dry every tear!

John the Beloved, gentle Apostle,
show us in vision the Lamb with his Bride,
arrayed for her Bridegroom, the Church in her
    splendor,
whose image is Mary, the Queen at his side.
Prophet of glory, pointing above,
guide us to heaven, home of God's love!

Priest of creation, Jesus all-holy,
come with your blessing to Cnoc's holy ground;
where once for our comfort you showed us your
    glory,
with praise and thanksgiving let Cnoc now
    resound.
Lamb of salvation, heaven's pure light,
lighten our darkness, banish our night!

Mother of Mercy

Irregular

Mother of mercy,
Queen of angels and Queen of saints,
joy of creation,
star of hope, we greet you.

Pity Eve's children,
pilgrims in exile from Eden;
in you we take refuge,
our comfort in sorrow,
sinless Eve, the world's true Mother.

Virgin Mary,
Queen of grace in glory,
pray for sinners,
lift up our hearts to things above,
in hope of heaven.

O Mary,
at the hour of death, our exile ended,
show us your Son, who is our peace,
our Savior.

Most holy,
most gracious,
most loving Mother of Jesus.

Text: James Quinn, SJ, ©.
Scripture References: st. 3: Rev. 19:7-8, 21:2-3;
    st. 4: Rev. 21:23
Topics: Biblical names (Joseph, John), Mary

Text: *Salve, regina;* trans. by James Quinn, SJ, ©.
Topics: Evening, Mary

O Mary, Conceived in the Grace of Your Son

11 11 11 11

O Mary, conceived in the grace of your Son,
the firstfruits of vict'ry on Calvary won!
he chose you as Mother to bring him to birth,
the one fitting shrine for his dwelling on earth!

Immaculate Virgin, with motherhood blest,
true God is the Child that in your womb did rest!
with you shall we ever Magnificat sing,
whose Son is our Maker and Savior and King!

O Mother, who stood by your Son till his death,
still stand by your children till life's dying breath!
O pray for us all as in glory you share
your Son's resurrection, his masterpiece fair!

Text: James Quinn, SJ, ©.
Possible Tune: JOANNA
Topics: Mary

O Queen of Heav'n, to You the Angels Sing

10 10 10 10

O Queen of heav'n, to you the angels sing,
the Maiden-Mother of their Lord and King;
O Woman raised above the stars, receive
the homage of your children, sinless Eve.

O full of grace, in grace your womb did bear
Emmanuel,. King David's promised heir;
O Eastern Gate, whom God had made his own,
by you God's glory came to Zion's throne.

O Burning Bush, you gave the world its light
when Christ your Son was born on Christmas
night;
O Mary Queen, who bore God's holy One,
for us, your children, pray to God your Son.

Text: *Ave, Regina caelorum;*
    trans. by James Quinn, SJ, ©.
Possible Tune: WOODLANDS
Topics: Evening, Mary

On Carmel's Mount Our Lady Tends

LM

On Carmel's mount Our Lady tends
a living garden rich in flowers;
God's Word has sown the seed of grace,
that grows in silent, prayer-filled hours.

In heaven's glory Carmel's saints
with Christ their King forever reign;
the firstborn Son enfolds in joy
his brethren, born of Mary's pain.

Dark night gives way to purest light,
the mystic sees with light unsealed;
the saints who bore Christ's wounds of love
now see Christ's wounds in love revealed.

The white-robed martyrs sing the praise
of Christ, the martyrs' glorious Lord;
the lowly now are lifted high,
to gain at last their great reward.

Give thanks to God, the fount of grace,
give thanks to God, our victim-priest,
give thanks to God, the breath of life,
for Carmel's saints on their great feast.

Text: James Quinn, SJ, ©.
Topics: Ascension, Mary, Saints

See from His Throne in Heav'n Above

CM

See, from his throne in heav'n above
God gazes down on earth,
to choose the Woman who will bring
the Prince of peace to birth.

He chooses one who will be born
to Joachim and Anne,
their child his fairest gift to earth
since life one earth began.

What joy now fills your loving hearts
as Mary, full of grace,
is born to you in Nazareth,
to be God's dwelling-place.

The sinless Eve brings God's own peace,
for she and she alone
has been conceived in grace, to be
God's Mother and our own.

Our heav'nly patrons, share with us
your deep humility,
which graced your child, the mystic rose,
the flower of Galilee.

Praise God, from whom all graces flow,
praise Mary's Child, his Son,
praise God the Spirit, sent by both,
with both for ever one.

A Sign Is Seen in Heaven

76 76D

A sign is seen in heaven,
a maiden-mother fair;
her mantle is the sunlight,
and stars adorn her hair.
the maiden's name is Mary;
in love she brings to birth
the Lord of all the ages,
the King of all the earth.

Like moonlight on the hilltops
she shines on all below;
like sunlight on the mountains
her Child outshines the snow.
O Mary, Queen of mothers,
still smile on young and old;
bless hearth and home and harvest;
bless farm and field and fold.

Pray, Mother, Queen in glory,
before the Father's throne;
praise God's eternal Wisdom,
the Child who is your own;
rejoice in God the Spirit,
whose power let you conceive
the Child of Eden's promise,
O new and sinless Eve.

Text: James Quinn, SJ, ©.
Possible Tune: DURROW
Scripture Reference: Revelation 12: 1-6, 17
Topics: Mary

Text: James Quinn, SJ, ©.
Topics: Mary

We Praise You, O Queen in Glory

88 76 78 78

We praise you, O queen in glory,
as above all the saints you reign;
we praise you, Nurse of Jesus,
of him who knew such pain.
You made yourself his handmaid
from manger to cruel death;
O Mary, still befriend us
as we breathe forth our dying breath.

When Adam and Eve were banished
from the Garden, and hope seemed dead,
God sent your Son, O Woman,
to crush the serpent's head.
The sinless Adam gave us
with John to the new Eve's care;
O sinless Eve, protect us,
Spotless Virgin beyond compare.

Text: James Quinn, SJ, ©.
Possible Tune: CEAD MOLADH LE MUIRE BHEANNAITHE
Topics: Mary

You Are All-Fair, O Mary of the Glories

11 10 11 10 D

You are all-fair, O Mary of the glories,
Daughter of Eve untouched by Adam's sin.
You are the flow'r of Zion, God's own city,
the everlasting joy of Israel.
You are the honor of God's holy people,
the patroness to whom we sinners turn.
Virgin most wise and Mother of compassion,
pray for us all to Jesus Christ, your Son, our Lord.

Who Is This in Glory Decked

77 77

Who is this in glory decked,
filling all the sky with light,
sun for mantle, stars for crown,
at her feet the silver moon?

This is Mary, sinless Eve,
she who brings God's Son to birth,
woman who in travail bears
sinless Adam's royal race.

Queen of angels, Queen of saints,
joy of heaven, star of hope,
Maiden-mother, full of grace,
pray for us in death's dark hour.

Text: James Quinn, SJ, ©.
Possible Tune: IS MAITH AN BHEAN MUIRE MHÓR
    (Trad. Irish)
Topics: Mary

Text: *Tota pulchra es;* trans. by James Quinn, SJ, ©.
Possible Tune: DERRY AIR
Topics: Mary

Five Sorrowful Mysteries of the Rosary

Garden
See the Lord weighed down by sin!
See the King bowed low to earth!
Abba, Father,
hear our prayer:
may your will, not ours, be done!
Ora, ora, ora, Maria!

Scourging at the Pillar
broken body, torn by sin,
may we share your pain and grief!
Wounded Jesus,
heal our wounds:
may we never sin again!
Ora, ora, ora, Maria!

Crowning with Thorns
see your King, your thorns his crown,
broken reed his royal power!
Man of sorrows,
break our pride!
Rule our hearts to make us free!
Ora, ora, ora, Maria!

Carrying of the Cross
Jesus bears our cross of sin!
See, he falls, to rise again!
"Come and follow!
"Walk with me!
"Share my cross, to share my crown!"
Ora, ora, ora, Maria!

Crucifixion
Christ has died that we may live!
Christ, our shepherd, saves his sheep!
Mother Mary,
Queen of grace,
stand by us when death is near!
Ora, ora, ora, Maria!

Five Joyful Mysteries of the Rosary

Annunciation
"Mary, sing with joyful heart:
"You shall bear Emmanuel!"
Virgin Mother
full of grace,
pray for us to God, your Son!
Ave, ave, ave, Maria!

Visitation
"Sing my soul, of God's great love!
Sing, my heart, your song of joy!
Praise his wonders,
praise his name,
praise his gift of God, my Son!"
Ave, ave, ave, Maria!

Nativity
Angels sing as shepherds watch:
"Praise to God, his peace on earth!
Christ the Savior,
Shepherd-King,
sleeps in straw in David's town!"
Ave, ave, ave, Maria!

Presentation
"Now I see the world's true light!
Glory shines on Israel!
God's great glory,
Christ the Lord,
comes to claim his dwelling-place!"
Ave, ave, ave, Maria!

Finding in the Temple
"Where is Jesus, child of grace?"
"Here, in God my Father's house!
"Where the Son is,
there is God!
"I am God's new house of prayer!"
Ave, ave, ave, Maria!

Text: James Quinn, SJ, ©.
Possible Tune: VIERGE SAINTE
Topics: Mary

Text: James Quinn, SJ, ©.
Possible Tune: VIERGE SAINTE
Topics: Mary

Glorious Mysteries of the Rosary

Resurrection
Alleluia! Sing for joy!
Jesus lives, to die no more!
King of Glory,
Risen Lord,
be our hope, our peace, our life!
Gaude, gaude, gaude, Maria!

Ascension
God the Father greets his Son,
Lord of lords and King of kings!
Priest in heaven,
Priest on earth,
make the whole creation one!
Gaude, gaude, gaude, Maria!

Coming of the Holy Spirit
Jesus sends from heaven's throne
God the Father's promised Gift!
Holy Spirit,
Bond of love,
come, and make God's children one!
Gaude, gaude, gaude, Maria!

Assumption of Our Lady into Heaven
See, a woman raised on high:
Mary, clothed in radiant light!
God's own Mother,
Sinless Eve,
enters into Paradise!
Gaude, gaude, gaude, Maria!

Coronation of Our Lady in Heaven
Glory fills the heav'nly court!
Angels bow before their Queen!
Queen of angels,
Queen of saints,
joy is yours for evermore!
Gaude, gaude, gaude, Maria!

Christ Is Victor

Christ is victor, Christ is ruler, Christ is Lord of all.

Christ, our King, hear us.
Christ, our King, hear us.
Bless and protect our Pope, the shepherd of all your
people. *Hear us.*
Grant to our bishop strength to sanctify, teach and
guide us. *Hear us.*
Strengthen in faith and love all bishops and priests
and deacons. *Hear us.*
Keep in your loving care your holy and faithful
people. *Hear us.*

Jesus, our Savior.
Strengthen and uphold us.
Mary, our Mother.
Strengthen and uphold us.
Peter, true shepherd.
Strengthen and uphold us.
Paul, fearless preacher.
Strengthen and uphold us.

John, priest and martyr.
Strengthen and uphold us.
Saints of our country.
Strengthen and uphold us.
Christ is victor, Christ is ruler, Christ is Lord of all.

Christ is Lord.

Christ is victor.
Christ is King.

Christ is ruler.
Christ reigns in glory.
Christ is Lord of all.
To him alone is the kingship, to him alone the
glory,
to him alone the pow'r throughout infinite ages.
Amen.
Christ is victor, Christ is ruler, Christ is Lord of all.

Text: James Quinn, SJ, ©.
Possible Tune: VIERGE SAINTE
Topics: Mary

Text: *Christus vincit* (Worcester antiphonary,
13th cent.); trans. by James Quinn, SJ, ©.
Possible Tune: CHRISTUS VINCIT
Topics: Church, King (Christ as), Saints

Christ Is Victor

Christ is victor, Christ is ruler, Christ is Lord of all.
Christ is victor, Christ is ruler, Christ is Lord of all.
Christ our King, hear us.
Christ our King, hear us.
Bless and protect our Pope, the shepherd of all your people.
Save him.

Jesus our Savior.
Strengthen and uphold him.
Mother of Jesus.
Strengthen and uphold him.
Peter, true shepherd.
Strengthen and uphold him.
Paul, fearless preacher.
Strengthen and uphold him.
Christ is victor, Christ is ruler, Christ is Lord of all.

Christ is Lord. *Christ is victor.*
Christ is King. *Christ is ruler.*
Christ reigns in glory. *Christ is Lord of all.*
To him alone is the kingship, to him alone the glory, to him alone the pow'r throughout infinite ages. Amen.
Christ is victor, Christ is ruler, Christ is Lord of all.

Christ Is Victor, Christ Is Ruler, Christ Is Lord of All

Christ is victor, Christ is ruler, Christ is Lord of all.
Christ is victor, Christ is ruler, Christ is Lord of all.

Lord Jesus, hear us.
Look kindly on us, your people, keep us in unity.
Lord Jesus, save us.
Protect and strengthen us. Mother of Jesus.
Protect and strengthen us. Husband of Mary
Protect and strengthen us. Michael, archangel.

Protect and strengthen us.
Christ is victor, Christ is ruler, Christ is Lord of all.

Lord Jesus, hear us.
Bless with wisdom and holiness our Pope and Shepherd, to guide your people.
Lord Jesus, save us.
Uphold and strengthen him.
Peter, shepherd.
Uphold and strengthen him.
Paul, wise teacher
Uphold and strengthen him.

Hosanna. *Hosanna.* Hosanna. *Son of the Father.*
Glory begotten of glory. *Almighty, eternal.*
Lord of all the ages.
Son of David, son of Abraham.
Shepherd-King of your people, Israel.

Lord Jesus, yesterday, today, and for ever.
Life, wisdom, and way to heaven.
Christ is victor, Christ is ruler, Christ is Lord of all.

Kingship, glory, and power are yours,
Spotless Lamb of sacrifice.,
Enthroned in splendor, age after age, for ever.
Amen.

Give to our world your gift of peace.
Lord, Jesus, prince of peace.
Redeemer Lord of creation. *Let justice rule.*
Let peace prevail. *Let love abound.*
Come, Lord Jesus, come in peace. Come Lord Jesus, come. Amen.

Text: *Christus vincit* (8th cent.);
    trans. by James Quinn, SJ, ©.
Possible Tune: CHRISTUS VINCIT
Topics: Easter

Text: *Christus vincit* (8th cent.);
    trans. by James Quinn, SJ, ©.
Topics: Church, King (Christ As), Guidance

Cry Out In Gladness, All the Earth
LMD

Cry out in gladness, all the earth,
acclaim the saint whose praise we sing,
who died a martyr, true as steel,
a faithful knight of Christ, his King.
St. John, from Scotland you embarked,
and travelled far your pilgrim way,
to find in Scotland's ancient faith
the light of everlasting day.

You found the City set on high,
the rock of faith the lamp of truth;
you vowed your life to Christ till death
with all the burning zeal of youth.
At last, to Scotland you returned,
a priest defying ruthless laws;
in chains, you preached the Church's faith,
and died upholding Peter's cause.

You loved God's mother: Mary's name
made holier still your dying breath;
you used her beads to win God's grace,
your parting gift in face of death.
The seed, though buried, yet will rise;
to bear its fruit, the grain has died:
may Scotland reap God's hundredfold,
the grace of Jesus crucified.

Like great Loyola you exchanged
your sword for Jesus' chivalry;
teach us to wield the Word of God,
the Spirit's sword, for unity.
in Heaven's glory pray that soon
our country may at last be one,
to preach on Gospel, break one Bread,
and be one Body in God's Son.

Let Carmel Echo Joyfully
LM

Let Carmel echo joyfully
the dying hymns that soared above
when Compiègne so gladly gave
its greatest witness to God's love.

These virgin-martyrs gave their lives
for sin's atonement, like their Lord;
they died to bring a troubled Church
the peace of Christ as love's reward.

May we like them serve Holy Church
and build it up in unity,
until at last in heav'n's pure light
we gaze on God the Trinity.

Our Queen and Mother, Carmel's joy,
look down with love on us who sing
the praise of those who died for love
of Jesus Christ, your Son, our King.

Bless God the Father, source of love,
bless God the Word, his only Son,
bless God the Spirit, Dove of peace,
one God, while endless ages run.

Text: James Quinn, SJ, ©.
Possible Tune: STRATHISLA
Topics: Biblical Names (John)

Text: James Quinn, SJ, ©.
Topics: Martyrs

Joseph, We Praise You
11 11 11 5

Joseph, we praise you, prince of God's own
household,
bearing the promise made of old to David,
chosen to foster Christ, the Lord's anointed,
Son of the Father.

Strong in your silence, swift in your obedience,
saving God's Firstborn when you fled from Herod,
cherish God's children as you cherished Jesus,
safe in your keeping.

Saint of the workbench, skilled and trusted
craftsman,
cheerfully toiling side by side with Jesus,
teach us to value lives of hidden splendor,
lived in God's presence.

Husband of Mary, one in joy and sorrow,
share with God's people love and peace and blessing;
may your example help our homes to mirror
Nazareth's glory.

Saint of the dying, when your work was ended
Jesus and Mary stood beside your deathbed;
so in life's evening may they stand beside you,
calling us homeward.

Lord Jesus Christ, You Built Your Church
8888 88

Lord Jesus Christ, you built your Church
on Peter's faith, not shifting sand;
on living rock, till time will end,
the Church will still unshaken stand.
Bless Peter's heir, whose see is Rome,
where all the world finds hearth and home.

You gave your flock to Peter's care,
and Peter's care will never cease;
another Peter feeds it still,
and leads it safe on paths of peace.
Make strong in faith your little flock,
to stand secure on Peter's rock.

Before you gave yourself in death,
you gave your Mother as our own;
may we, her children, grow in grace,
to live, like her, for you alone.
Bless him to whom heav'n's keys are giv'n,
true son of Mary, Queen of heav'n.

Throughout the world your Church is one
in faith, in hope, in charity;
the Church at Rome presides in love,
the sign, the seal, of unity.
Be with our world, its only hope;
be with your Church; be with our Pope.

Text: James Quinn, SJ, ©.
Possible Tune: MELITA
Scripture References: st. 1, Matthew 7:24-27; st. 2, John
21:15-17; st. 3, 19:25-27, Matthew 16:19
Topics: Church

Text: James Quinn, SJ, ©.
Possible Tune: ISTE CONFESSOR
Topics: Biblical Names (Joseph)

O First Among
the Chosen Twelve
CM

O first among the chosen Twelve
once Simon, Son of John,
you now are named the living Rock
on whom the Church is built.

"Your name is Peter," said Our Lord,
"On you I build my Church;
no power of death can overthrow
what stands upon this Rock."

"With you I leave the keys of heav'n,
to open and to close;
what you will bind is bound by God;
what you will loose is loosed."

"The Evil One has sought you out
to winnow you like wheat,
but I have prayed for rock-like faith,
that you may strengthen all."

"You love me, Simon, more than these?"
three times the Shepherd asked;
"Yes, Lord," you said; and he replied:
"Then feed my lambs, my sheep."

You are the Church's living Rock;
on you we rest secure.
You are the Shepherd of the flock;
still shepherd us in love.

Saint Augustine,
Wisest Preacher
887D

Saint Augustine, wisest Preacher,
still be with us as our teacher,
guide our feet on wisdom's guest.
Restless mind, by Wisdom captured,
Soaring Spirit, love enraptured,
lead us where our hearts find rest.

Troubled heart, you long resisted
Wisdom's claim, and still insisted
on your freedom, but in vain.
Children's voices gaily singing,
kept within your mem'ry ringing;
"Take and read": God's will was plain.

Word made flesh, your heart inflaming,
mother's tears, your own tears claiming,
showed you God, the good, the true.
Late you loved his ancient splendor,
late you found in love's surrender
beauty old, yet ever new.

Rapt in loving contemplation,
with new eyes you saw creation,
bathed with glory from above.
Deep you drank from Wisdom's fountain,
high you climbed the mystic's mountain
to the vision of God's love.

Glory be to God, excelling
all that is, in glory dwelling
with his Wisdom, God the Son.
Glory be to God, proceeding
from their love, to all truth leading
those who in his Truth are one.

Text: James Quinn, SJ, ©.
Possible Tune: ST. PETER
Topics: Biblical names (Peter), Church

Text: James Quinn, SJ, ©.
Possible Tune: STABAT MATER + AUSTIN

Saint of Siena, Fed by God
LM

Saint of Siena, fed by God
with hidden manna from above,
teach us to walk his ways of peace,
and learn the secrets of his love.

Prophet of God, on fire with zeal
for holy Church, his dwelling-place,
pray that his Word may bathe the world
in all the splendor of his grace.

Saint of the Church, you strove to bring
its shepherd home to Peter's see:
teach us to look to Peter's heir
for truth, for strength, for unity.

Saint of the lowly, pray that we
may see the greatest in the least,
and share the Banquet of the poor
as Wisdom's guests at Wisdom's feast.

Saint of the Cross, for love you bore
the glorious wounds of Christ our Lord:
help us to bear his cross of pain
that we may share his great reward.

Daughter of God, the Spirit's breath
inspired your love for God the Son;
so now in glory's vision sing
the praise of God, for ever one.

Sing, Francis
10 10 10 10

Refrain
Sing, Francis, sing a song for our today,
sing us the song that you would have us sing:
sing us the song of all that you hold dear,
of love and peace , of joy in everything.

My song is love, the love of Christ my Lord,
my song is joy, the joy of heav'n above,
my song is peace, that only God can give,
my song is God, my everlasting love.

My song the sun, our brother in the sky,
my song the moon, our sister of the night,
my song the stars, that shine around God's throne,
my song the earth, her creatures my delight.
   Refrain

I sing the praise of Lady Poverty,
who made me rich when I became her slave;
I sing of him who stripped himself of all,
and rose as Lord in triumph from the grave.

I sing of One who freed me from myself,
who breathed on me and new life filled my soul,
who kissed my wounds and cured their leprosy,
who gazed on me and, smiling, made me whole.
   Refrain

I sing of wounds that heal the wounded world,
of heart once pierced, from which my heart was
     born,
of hands outstretched embracing all the earth,
of feet once kissed, which cruel nails have torn.

My song is pain, the pain of Christ my Lord,
my song is heav'n, where seraphs sing his praise,
my song is death, the friend who leads me home,
my song is life, true life for endless days.

Text: James Quinn, SJ, ©.
Topics: Saints

Text: James Quinn, SJ, ©.
Possible Tune: PAX FRANCIS
Topics: St. Francis of Assisi

St. Cecilia, Loving Patron
87 87

St. Cecilia, loving Patron,
look on us who look at you:
as you sing God's praise in heaven
pray for us, our faith renew.

St. Cecilia, glorious martyr,
by the blood you shed in death
keep us true by your example,
true to Christ till life's last breath.

St. Cecilia, wisest virgin,
teach us where to find true love;
teach us Mary's song of gladness,
which she sings in heav'n above.

St. Cecilia, music's patron,
alleluia is your song;
keep our voices tuned to heaven,
where our hearts and minds belong.

Glory be to God the Father,
glory be to Christ, the Son,
glory be to God, their Spirit,
persons three, for ever one.

Text: James Quinn, SJ, 1993, ©.
Topics: Alleluias, Music, Saints

Topical Index

113

Scriptural Index

115

Metrical Index

Index of Translations by Original Title or First Line

Index of First Lines and Titles

www.ingramcontent.com/pod-product-compliance
Ingram Content Group UK Ltd.
Pitfield, Milton Keynes, MK11 3LW, UK
UKHW031249020325
455689UK00008B/158